P9-DWK-208

Dear You,

My name is Carrie and I'm twenty-two years old. Apparently that makes me an adult. Yikes. *hides stuffed animals*

Anyhow, grown up or not, I did manage to make it through the "Teen Age" more or less in one piece and, a few years ago, I started talking and writing online about some of the things I learned back then . . . and a few things I've realized since. My daft videos and blogs about broken hearts, bullies, and body image—among other things—seemed to help people, so I collected all those thoughts and bits of advice and ramblings into a book. This book. And gosh, isn't it pretty? Go on, stroke it. You know you want to.

I'm not an expert on "life" (things I am an expert on: cake, Disney, making the perfect cuppa—that's about it), but I think I do know a bit about what's worrying you* and maybe, with a little bit of luck, some of my stories will make you smile, make you think, and, most of all, give you faith that it will all work out all right in the end. Because it will. Promise. *All I Know Now* is not all that much, but I hope it's enough to help.

Lots of love,

xxx

*Everything, right?

Praise for CARRIE HOPE FLETCHER
and *All I Know Now*

#1 *Sunday Times* bestseller (UK)

"Oh, what a fantastic book—so honest, so brilliant, so *kind*."
—**Jill Mansell**, author of *Don't Want to Miss a Thing*

"Full of warmth, wit, and wisdom, [Carrie is] the big sister
everyone needs."—*Top of the Pops* magazine

"Being picked on at school certainly hasn't held Carrie Hope
Fletcher back . . . she radiates openness, sparky humor, and a
self-possession far beyond her years."—*Daily Mail* (UK)

"[She's] young, fab, and incredibly talented. I think I manage to
keep my massive jealousy of Carrie Hope Fletcher just [barely]
under control :-)."—**Jenny Colgan**, author of *West End Girls*
and *The Little Beach Street Bakery*

"Oh @CarrieHFletcher I am *loving* your book. You are wise
beyond your years."—**Harriet Evans**, author of *A Place for Us*

"*All I Know Now* is exactly what my teenage self needed, and
a reminder for my 26-year-old self that we're not alone in our
quirks, breaks, wonder, and woes . . . it's absolutely magic."
—**Jodi Ann Bickley**, author of *One Million Lovely Letters*

"Carrie has written the ultimate life survival guide
for teens and beyond!"—**Ali McNamara**,
author of *From Notting Hill with Love . . . Actually*

THE EXPERIMENT

BECAUSE EVERY BOOK IS A TEST OF NEW IDEAS

"It's super mega awesome."
—**Emma Blackery**, YouTube.com/EmmaBlackery

Why fans love
CARRIE HOPE FLETCHER

"I love Carrie because she taught me that it's okay
to just be me."—**Felicia Hu,** @treehuggerluna

"Carrie feels like the big sister I always wanted and needed. Her
laughter is infectious, she's daring and driven, and she can make
me crack a smile even on the darkest of days. Carrie is relatable,
genuine, and inspiring in more ways than one."—**Holly Platts**

"Carrie's like a kind, caring, and witty big sister. If you've
ever got a worry about anything, she always has a wise and
hopeful word to share."—**Alice Rose,** @ajrose86

"I love Carrie because she made me realize that it's okay to be a
little weird and crazy as long as I'm myself."—**Emma Hawkins**

"Carrie makes me smile and she makes me think. She makes
me feel like being me is the most awesome thing in the universe.
I love her because she makes me love this world and myself a
bit more."—**Liv Conrad**

All I Know Now

Albany County
Public Library
Laramie, Wyoming

All I Know Now

WONDERINGS **AND** ADVICE ON
Making Friends, Making Mistakes,
Falling in (and Out of) Love, and Other
Adventures in Growing Up Hopefully

WRITTEN AND ILLUSTRATED BY

Carrie Hope Fletcher

THE EXPERIMENT
NEW YORK

ALL I KNOW NOW: *Wonderings and Advice on Making Friends, Making Mistakes, Falling in (and Out of) Love, and Other Adventures in Growing Up Hopefully*

Text and illustrations copyright © 2015 Carrie Hope Fletcher
Excerpt on page 141 from **"Thank Goodness"**
from the Broadway Musical WICKED
Music and Lyrics by Stephen Schwartz
Copyright © 2003 Grey Dog Music
All Rights Reserved   Used by Permission
Reprinted by Permission of Hal Leonard Corporation

Originally published in Great Britain in 2015 by Sphere, an imprint of Little, Brown Book Group.

All rights reserved. Except for brief passages quoted in newspaper, magazine, radio, television, or online reviews, no portion of this book may be reproduced, distributed, or transmitted in any form or by any means, electronic or mechanical, including photocopying, recording, or information storage or retrieval system, without the prior written permission of the publisher.

Many of the designations used by manufacturers and sellers to distinguish their products are claimed as trademarks. Where those designations appear in this book and The Experiment was aware of a trademark claim, the designations have been capitalized.

The Experiment's books are available at special discounts when purchased in bulk for premiums and sales promotions as well as for fund-raising or educational use. For details, contact us at info@theexperimentpublishing.com.

The Experiment, LLC
220 East 23rd Street, Suite 301
New York, NY 10010-4674
www.theexperimentpublishing.com

Library of Congress Cataloging-in-Publication Data

Fletcher, Carrie Hope.
  All I know now : wonderings and advice on making friends, making mistakes, falling in (and out of) love, and other adventures in growing up hopefully / Carrie Hope Fletcher.
     pages cm
   ISBN 978-1-61519-294-6 (pbk.) -- ISBN 978-1-61519-295-3 (ebook)
1. Teenagers--Life skills guides--Juvenile literature. 2. Teenagers--Conduct of life--Juvenile literature. 3. Success in adolescence--Juvenile literature. I. Title.
   HQ796.F667 2015
   305.235--dc23
                                    2015020470

ISBN 978-1-61519-294-6
Ebook ISBN 978-1-61519-295-3

Cover design by Sarah Smith
Author photograph copyright © Charlie Hopkinson
Original text design by M Rules
Additional text design by Sarah Schneider

Manufactured in the United States of America
Distributed by Workman Publishing Company, Inc.
Distributed simultaneously in Canada by Thomas Allen & Son Ltd.

First printing August 2015
10 9 8 7 6 5 4 3 2 1

This book is for those
who said I'd never
get anywhere in life
and those who never
doubted for a second
that I would.
Without either of you,
I wouldn't be here.

Thank you.

Program

Prologue: Getting to Know Me   1

Overture: All I Know Now   11

ACT 1 How to Make Friends Without Vomiting on Their Shoes . . . and Other School Stories

1: Firsts   19

2: Making Friends   35

3: Work Versus Play   43

4: Asking Questions   47

5: Making Mistakes   51

6: How to Apologize   55

ACT 2 Not Everyone Is Going to Like You . . . and Why That Doesn't Matter!

7: Hindsight   67

8: How to Handle a Bully   77

9: How to Identify If You're a Bully   83

10: The Rumor Mill   93

11: The Art of Biting Your Tongue   97

ACT 3 How to Get Your Heart Broken Only Just a Little Bit

12: The Disgusting Business of
Falling in Love   103

13: The Birds and the Bees   107

14: Let Yourself Feel Pretty   119

15: Happy and Healthy   123

16: How NOT to Handle a Break-Up   129

17: Losing What You Never Had   135

18: Dating Myself   137

19: The Idea of Love   141

ACT 4 The Internet: It's More Than Just Lolcatz

20: Internetiquette   147

21: Jeez, It's Just My Opinion!   153

22: The Twitter-Sphere   157

23: How to Call Someone Out   165

24: How to Deal with Being
Called Out   169

25: Online Versus IRL   173

Intermission   177

ACT 5 People: Imagining Them Complexly

26: Onions   181
27: The Right Way   187
28: Journeys   193
29: Living with Yourself   195
30: Houses   201
31: Nobody's Perfect   207

ACT 6 I Dreamed a Dream

32: Unrealistic   215
33: Being Realistic   219
34: Dreams Change   223
35: In It to Win It   227
36: Possibilities   231

ACT 7 Turning That Frown Upside Down

37: Nice for No Reason   237
38: You Get What You Give   241
39: Creating Your Own Misery   245
40: Choosing to Be Happy   251
41: Not to Worry   255
42: Hurting Yourself   259

ACT 8 Life: Proud Parents, Flimsy Fibs, and Peaceful Pasts

43: Fibs   265
44: The Parentals   269
45: Soul Shrapnel   275
46: Ripples   279
47: It's Not All About You   283
48: Choices   285
49: "It's Easier Said Than Done!"   287
50: The Past and Making Peace with It   291
51: #AskCarrie   297

Finale   313
Props (aka all the useful phone numbers
 and websites you might need)   317
Curtain Call   333
Find Me Online!   337
About the Author   338

PROLOGUE

Getting to Know Me

I am, first and foremost, above all else, an actress and a singer, destined to spend my life in the spotlight, on stage and screen in front of crowds of people. I regularly make videos and share them with thousands of people online. But, believe it or not, I don't actually like attention. I don't really like talking about myself. So then how do I tell you about who I am, what I do, and why you should read my book without dying of cringe? Well, I thought I'd give that job to the people I trust most: my friends, family, and colleagues. They probably know me better than I know myself, so I set them a little quiz. If you've been watching my videos for a while, turn the page to see how many of these questions you know the answer to, and read on to see how my nearest and dearest fared.

HOW WELL DO YOU KNOW CARRIE?

1.   *Why is my YouTube channel called ItsWayPastMyBedtime?*

2.   *What common household item do I hold in all of my videos?*

3.   *Who would be my three dream dinner-party guests?*

4.   *Which of these is not the title of one of my videos?*

     a) Leaping into the Unknown
     b) Why I Hate Tea and Cake!
     c) The One Where I Pee in a Onesie

5.   *What color are my eyes?*

6. *Which cereal advert did I appear in as a child?*

7. *Complete this line from my song, "Boys in Books Are Better":*

And you could take me _____ if you've
been made up by _____ .

8. *What was the first video I posted on YouTube?*

a) A cover of "On My Own" from *Les Misérables*
b) A cover of "Defying Gravity" from *Wicked*
c) A cover of "The Only Exception" by Paramore

9. *What is my favorite book?*

10. *What do my subscribers call themselves?*

Here are Celinde Schoenmaker, my good friend from Theaterland; Tom Fletcher, my brother; and Pete Bucknall from the YouTube world to answer my quiz questions. (For all the CORRECT answers, please turn to page 10.)

1. *Why is my YouTube channel called ItsWayPastMyBedtime?*

Celinde: I want to say, because of a song? Because I think I heard that once . . . but now I say it I'm not sure, and I want to say: because the first video you uploaded was way past your bedtime and you were like . . . BINGO!   ✗

Tom: Because you're much better at thinking of YouTube channel names than your brother aka TomMcFlyTwitter/Tomplicated ✗

Pete: Something about something you had to do with a flying car . . . I think . . . maybe.   ✓

Close enough, Pete!

2. *What common household item do I hold in all of my videos?*

Celinde: Come on . . . a cup of tea! Easy. ;-)   ✓

Tom: Toothbrush? A mug? A cuddly toy?! Paper! Snow! A ghost! ✗

Pete: Often . . . MY *Nightmare Before Christmas* mug! But always some sort of ceramic tea-holding device.   ✓

3. *Who would be my three dream dinner party guests?*

Celinde: Rapunzel, Stitch, and Elsa. Or do you mean real people? 'Cause then I think it would be . . . Buzz, J.K. Rowling, and Walt Disney. ✗

Tom: I don't know, but if I were one of them and you didn't invite Natalie Portman as one of your remaining two guests I would pick up my plate and eat my vegan sausages in the other room. ✗

Pete: Me (obviously), James McAvoy, and perhaps Chinese Emperor Shen Nung? (The inventor of tea!) Failing that . . . Walt Disney. ✗

Great guest choices! But not quite . . .

4. *Which of these is not the title of one of my videos?*

    (a) Leaping into the Unknown
    (b) Why I Hate Tea and Cake!
    (c) The One Where I Pee in a Onesie

Celinde: "Why I Hate Tea and Cake!" Because you definitely do not hate tea and cake! Peeing in a onesie . . . I mean, I can see you doing that. ✓

Tom: I have absolutely no idea, I only watch the ones that say "Dear Tom" in the title. ;-) ✗
RUDE!

Pete: AS IF you would ever make a video called "Why I Hate Tea and Cake!" Talk about blasphemy! ✓

5. *What color are my eyes?*

Celinde: Brown! ✓

Tom: They are all brown. ✓

Pete: Think of the color of the nicest, richest, warmest chocolate cake you can . . . and there you go! ✓

6. *Which cereal advert did I appear in as a child?*

Celinde: I have seen it, but come on, Carrie, I'm Dutch! The only one I know is Kellogg's . . . so I will say that one? ✗

Tom: You were the monkey in the Coco-Pops adverts before your tail removal surgery. You were also Little Red Riding Hood in the Honey Nut Cheerios advert.

So many questions! Is there a prize at the end of this or some sort of certificate at least? ✓

Pete: Honey Nut Cheerios! Which weirdly enough, I saw when I was a kid . . . Destiny! ✓

7. *Complete this line from my song, "Boys in Books Are Better":*

And you could take me _____ if you've been made up by _____ .

Celinde: Rowing, Rowling (if this is actually true can I please be rewarded for this)?   ½

So close, Celinde!

Tom: And you could take me to—the library if you've been made up by shmir . . . shmibrary?   ✗

Pete: And you could take me something something boys in books! If you've been made up by something something lalalala they're better!   ✗

8. *What was the first video I posted on YouTube?*

(a) A cover of "On My Own" from *Les Misérables*
(b) A cover of "Defying Gravity" from *Wicked*
(c) A cover of "The Only Exception" by Paramore

Celinde: A cover of "On My Own" from *Les Misérables*   ✗ because I want this to be true . . . wouldn't that be amazing.

Tom: Trick question! It's actually secret answer (d) a cover of "U Can't Touch This" by MC Hammer, which was later removed due to your rapping skills being too fresh.   ✗

Pete: (I definitely didn't have to search that . . .) It was "The Only Exception!" Although I heard your cover of "On My Own" first! ✓

9. *What is my favorite book?*

Celinde: You say this about so many books! I think you loved *One Day*, *All My Friends Are Superheroes,* and *The Fault in Our Stars*. I can't pick one. Wait, what about *this* one?! This should be your favorite book! ✓

Tom: I'm pretty sure it's *The Dinosaur That Pooped Christmas* . . . or maybe it's *The Dinosaur That Pooped the Past* . . . definitely one of those. Maybe. ✗

Pete: The last time I checked . . . it was *All My Friends Are Superheroes* by Andrew Kaufman. (P.S. Thank you for telling me about it! What a book!) ✓

10. *What do my subscribers call themselves?*

Celinde: HOPEFULS! (PINKY.) ✓

Tom: Hoperers . . . no, wait . . . I know this, hopeless? Hmmmm, hoppers? Hopey people? Hopefuls! ✓

Pete: The Hopefuls. The most loyal, kind, caring subscribers I have ever seen. ✓

And bonus round: What is the best and worst thing about me?

Celinde: Worst thing would be: You seduce me with sweets when I'm sitting there with two eggs and half an avocado trying to be healthy . . . And you know it!

Best thing: You're this incredible little explosion of talent, love, and friendship! You inspire so many people, and it's an absolute joy to be around your positive vibes (and fabulous hair)! With big laughs from the beginning, and more laughs to come, and I can't wait. My little Carrie fairy, don't ever change. Lots of love.

Tom: I imagine the best thing is that the largeness of your hair means you never need to pack a pillow when camping. The worst thing . . . you smell funny.

Pete: The Best: Once you have made a decision, there's no changing your mind.

The Worst: Once you have made a decision . . . there's no changing your mind!

Aww, guys! Points all round!

And the winner is . . .

PETE!

QUIZ ANSWERS

1. My YouTube channel is called ItsWayPastMyBedtime because it came from a line in *Chitty Chitty Bang Bang*, which I was in as a child. Each night Grandpa Potts would say to Jeremy and Jemima "It's 20:32, it's way past your bedtime." Which also explains why my second channel on YouTube is called TwentyThirtyTwo!

2. A mug of tea.

3. Johnny Depp, Gerard Way, and Walt Disney!

4. Why I Hate Tea and Cake.

5. My eyes are brown.

6. I was in an advert for Honey Nut Cheerios, appearing as Little Red Riding Hood!

7. "And you could take me **bowling** if you were made up by **Rowling**."

8. The first video I posted on YouTube was a cover of "The Only Exception" by Paramore.

9. My favorite book is *All My Friends Are Superheroes* by Andrew Kaufman.

10. My subscribers call themselves Hopefuls!

OVERTURE

All I Know Now

I DON'T KNOW WHAT I'M DOING. In life, in love, in work, in general. *I just don't know what I'm doing.* I'm making it up as I go along. Doing it on the fly. Winging it. Haven't a clue. I am not qualified, in any way, to be telling you how to live your life. I'm a singing, acting, stumbling, bumbling London girl who's led rather a daft life. I don't have a degree in anything. I didn't even train to sing or act. I've learned what I've learned through living my life, knocking things over, breaking things, fixing them, and learning how not to do the same thing again—hopefully. I've made mistakes. Loads of 'em. More mistakes than I have fingers and toes . . . twice over. And I hope that reading about some of my mistakes will help you avoid your own—or if not avoid, at least handle them a little better. At the very least, I hope these stories from my life will make you smile (and/or wet yourself laughing at what a massive dork I am).

I was lucky enough to have a really amazing childhood. My mum and dad were very grounded and incredibly supportive and really made sure that my brother and I were as happy as we could be. My brother, being seven years older than I am, was also very protective and was always looking out for me. It's fair to say, though, that I was a bit of an imp when I was younger. I used to play this game called "Run Away Cheeky" . . . which basically entailed me yelling "RUN AWAY CHEEKY!" to my parents, legging it, and hiding from them. How my parents managed to survive bringing me up is truly beyond me. Well done, the both of you!

I was in three West End shows before the age of eleven, but my parents made sure none of it went to my head, so I think I've turned into a *relatively* normal adult. (I say "relatively" because how normal are any of us, really?) But despite getting off to a pretty good start in life, like many people I began to struggle in my teenage years. I'm a pretty dramatic girl at the best of times, but if you mix that into a huge cauldron with a million and one hormones, the pressure to pass exams with good marks, the constant chase to find a boyfriend more quickly than your peers (which then conflicts with your desperate need to fit in with them all), keeping up with the latest fashions (even if you don't like them)—and unless you're one of the *few* lucky ones (and I wasn't)—being bullied on top of it all, then . . . *Bibbidi-bobbidi-boo!* You get a rather confused, panicky teenager who is just about ready to pull the duvet up over her head and refuse to leave the house ever again.

When I was in the "Teen Age," I was never sure whether I was "normal" or not. I never seemed to swap my number with any boys at school dances, I never really enjoyed the shopping trips my friends organized because we ended up in Abercrombie & Fitch rather than Waterstones. And then when we were about fifteen they all seemed to start smoking, and that was so not what I was into . . . and yet I *thought* I respected my friends and their choices, so what was I missing? How was I supposed to dress and act to get boys' MSN addresses? And was I supposed to like all the things my friends liked? Or should I at least pretend to fit in? And is drinking a rite of passage? Or can I opt out without looking like a wuss? Does any of this sound familiar to you? If it does, it certainly makes me feel better. I wasn't such a weirdo after all, and I hope it makes you feel that you aren't, either!

All this hindsight is all very well and good, but at the time, all of those questions drove me to the point of questioning my entire existence and my purpose on this earth. (Told you I was dramatic.) In the end, I pushed and persevered through the crap all teenagers go through. The bullying, the mistakes, the arguments, the dates, the boys, the sex, the peer pressure, the crushes, the friends, the enemies, the frenemies . . . and now I'm here. Here watching you guys go through almost identical experiences and panicking just like I panicked. I'm watching from afar, trapped on the wrong side of a computer screen. Helpless . . . until now.

When I was a growing up, there were times when I wished I had a manual. A handbook that told me exactly how to avoid the stupid situations I got myself into, or how to get myself *out* of the ones I was already in. But there wasn't one. At the same time, I felt like there was a lack of role models for people my age, male or female. Maybe I just wasn't searching hard enough, and maybe I didn't need to, as I had always looked up to my big brother Tom for advice and guidance. He served as role model enough. (Showing me how best to wind up my parents, how to heat up "too cold" ice cream in the microwave, and how you know that, when the burgers are on fire, they're done.) I know that you guys are looking for advice and role models too—whether they're celebrities, singers, actors, reality TV stars or YouTubers/vloggers. Somehow, slowly, over my few years online making videos—talking about my rather daft life and telling stories to whoever is bored on a Sunday afternoon—I've made something of a name for myself as an "honorary big sister." I don't pretend or even think or feel like I'm an expert or someone who's studied, well . . . anything! I'm not a doctor or a professor, and I don't have two qualifications to rub together, but I do feel—as someone who has stood exactly where you guys are standing now—that I have a pretty good idea of how I can help. My inbox is filled to the brim, daily, with questions that the askers wouldn't dare discuss with their parents, teachers, or other authority figures that they find scary. You turn to me, us, the generation of vloggers and bloggers, because we're close enough in age that you know we understand and you feel like you know us so well (because of the amount of our lives, experiences, and stories we share with you) but we're still distant and removed enough from your situations for you not to feel too exposed when confiding in us about your deepest, darkest issues. You feel somewhat anonymous, and therefore you open up more and aren't as scared to ask for help.

So this is why I had the idea to write the manual I yearned for when I was a teenager. In these pages, you'll read about all the really stupid things I've done wrong and what I learned from them, in the hopes that you'll learn from them too, and that my tales of woe will make you laugh, make you think, and, maybe, help you if you find yourself on the verge of making a similar mistake. That's not to say I think making a mistake is bad. Quite the opposite; mistakes can be brilliant! Make as many as you like, because no matter how similar our problems, our mistakes will always be different and unique to us, and you'll learn things from them that have never even occurred to me. And maybe in years to come, YOU can write a book about it to help the generation behind you. But this is me: my story, my mistakes, and my lessons learned. I clawed my way out of the Teen Age with very little help—not because it wasn't offered, but because I was too stupid to ask for it. So, now that I've emerged on the other side and I'm doing OK, I'm turning around and helping pull other people through. I'm giving you the chance to seek help without having to ask for it. All you need to do is *read*.

ACT 1

*How to Make
Friends Without
Vomiting on
Their Shoes . . .
and Other
School Stories*

1

Firsts

First chapter, Carrie. Gotta make it good. You need to talk about something with substance. You've actually got to have a topic, Carrie. Something with some real meaning that these people will want to read about. If this first chapter is average or just plain bad, the rest of the book from here on out will be pointless. Start as you mean to go on, Carrie. Yes?

NO, INNER CRITIC. Shush, just . . . shush. I don't know about you, but I've had enough of people putting so much pressure on "firsts." Whether it's the first comment on a YouTube video, your first day at a new school or new job, or your first sexual experience, there is just too much unnecessary pressure! I had a thirteen-year-old girl ask me, on the wonderful world of Tumblr, if there was something wrong with her because she didn't have a boyfriend yet. I calmly explained that she was still so young, with her whole life ahead of her, and told her that I didn't find my first proper boyfriend until I was sixteen. But in my head I was screaming, "You're thirteen!" When I was thirteen, all I cared about was whether there would be cheesecake after lunch at school! It freaked me out that she didn't think boys were smelly, under-evolved creatures who burped and farted and left trails of slime wherever they went. Hell, I'm twenty-two and I still think that!

In those early teen years, around eleven to thirteen, adulthood and responsibility start paying an interest in you. You can feel them following not far behind, lurking behind bushes and buildings, leering at you, and it's a horrible feeling you just can't shake. It feels like there are so many things hurtling toward you that you've never experienced before, and you don't know if you're equipped to handle them. First day of high school, college, or a job, first boyfriend, first kiss, first . . . stuff that follows kisses (I blushed, I'll admit it) and SO MANY MORE. "You might as well just give up now!" says the mean Inner Critic in your head. But you shouldn't give up because when you're *that* side of the giant chasm that is teenage life, all the obstacles seem HUGE like those massive red balls in *Total Wipeout*. But looking back at them from this side, they're merely those bouncy balls you rode on in Pre-K, and getting over them wasn't nearly as hard as you thought it'd be. Although, there's no telling that to my thirteen-year-old self because she worries about everything.

So, what's my point?

Firsts aren't nearly as important as we make them.

There are a lot of different firsts a person can have, but in those early teenage years there are two main ones that seem rather daunting and overpowering, so I'm going to focus on those.

SCHOOL

Your first day is, most likely, not just *your* first day. You're in with a whole class or grade who are also feeling the same pressure and anxieties that you are, so my tip is: Don't underestimate how self-involved people can be when nervous. Look around at everyone else in the room. How much do you care about what they're doing? Or what they look like? Are you secretly hoping they'll show themselves up? I can bet the answer is no, not at all, because you're only thinking about YOU. And too right! It's a big day for you, and you need to be self-aware, but never forget that everyone else is also feeling the same way about themselves. No one is even thinking about you, let alone watching you and waiting for you to screw up. Think about how you're feeling: *What if I make a mistake? Do I look OK? Am I having a bad hair day? How can I get through this? What if no one likes me? Me, me, me!* Everyone else is feeling exactly the same things about *themselves*. Not you. They all think they're standing alone on a stage in the spotlight and everyone else is in the crowd, scrutinizing their every move, when really we're ALL standing on the stage, but the lights are off and there's no one left in the audience to watch you. The only pressure to make a good impression and be memorable is coming from yourself, so take the heat off a little bit. Also, if it's any comfort, your first day at school probably won't be as difficult as *my* first day at school . . .

My First Day at School

I was in a production of *Mary Poppins* in Bristol for the very first two months of my new high school. I didn't get away with not being tutored, though—I was sent all my textbooks and workbooks, and the nine other children in the show and I had a personal tutor to help us along. Being in the show was so much fun, but it meant that my first day at my actual, proper school was two months after everyone else's, and I was terrified to discover just how much I'd missed. Work-wise, of course, but more importantly to twelve-year-old me, socially. The school was a rather large one with around eight hundred girls from the ages of three to eighteen—I felt like a little tadpole in an ocean. I walked into a classroom full of kids who had already decided who was cool and who wasn't, what the cliques were and who was in them, and who sat where at lunchtime in the cafeteria. Everyone already knew that they could get away with not wearing their blazers, that they could roll their skirts up so they hung just *above* the knee, and that the rule about having *only black* school bags was more like a guideline and not something that would land you in detention. All of this had been learned while I was away.

So, in I walked, through the blue school gates, in my blue blazer that was a little on the large side with a five-pound note from my dad in the inside pocket, an exceedingly long skirt swaying way past my knees, and my hefty black rucksack that made me look like a gothic turtle, not knowing what clique I'd fit into, or even if I was going to fit into any.

I'm not going to lie or sugar-coat it . . . it was terrifying. It always is when you walk into a room full of peers you don't know, all of them ogling you like you're a bridge troll that's just swaggered in trailing a length of moss and slime with cat skulls tangled in its weeds. For me, it was particularly scary because, as I'd gathered from the girl who'd been sent to meet me from the school office, all the girls had long ago been told I had been in a show and that I was "Tom from McFly's sister." Snap judgments of me had been made instantly, and I didn't realize until I walked into my form room just how hard it would be to change their minds after they'd lived with that image of me in their heads for so long. Making friends comes naturally to some, but I always used to be a little uncertain of how to approach people (and if you are like I was, keep reading—there's a chapter for us later!) but, believe me, it's even harder to make friends when they've all decided what sort of person you are before you've even said hello.

I bet she's really stagey. A proper theater snob!

I bet she thinks she's better than everyone because her brother's in a famous band.

I bet she's on the verge of a nervous breakdown because she's got pushy parents!

How do you even begin to break down those judgments and prove to your peers that you're just a normal, nervous girl in year seven, trying to make friends? It's extremely hard, I'll tell you that for free!

In the midst of this generally petrifying day, the few friendly faces I saw shone out like beacons. When I sat down in one of my first classes, the girl in front of me, who had golden skin, dark brown hair, and the sort of cheeks you just want to pinch between your fingers, turned around and said, "Harriet, can I borrow a pencil?"

"Harriet?" she said a little louder, and when I didn't answer . . . "HARRIET!"

I finally looked up but, as I did, the girl sitting at the desk next to me gently told the girl in front, "Erm, her name's Carrie."

Instead of looking mortified, like I expected, she burst into a fit of giggles and introduced herself as Saffron. I can't tell you how relieved I was. But truth be told, the friendly faces were in the minority. I had to do that awful clichéd introduction that schools usually make you do when you're "the new girl." They made me stand in front of the class and state my name and "a little bit about myself." When I sat back down, a little flushed and flustered, the girl to my right sidled up to me and said, "So, can you get me free McFly tickets?" This was a situation I'd been in all too frequently at my primary school, so I knew my correct response was to shake my head and to ignore "those sorts of people." I felt like Harry Potter when Draco Malfoy tells him he doesn't want to be making friends with "the wrong sort." Thankfully, like Harry, I could tell the wrong sort for myself! Later on, after lunchtime when the bell had rung, signaling that we all had to make our way to our next class, and I had my books ready for the last four lessons of the day, I walked through my form room doorway only to trip over a well-placed foot in the hall.

"Whoops! Was that me?" The same girl grinned as she strutted off, leaving me and my books strewn across the hallway in front of the upper-school girls who were lined up waiting to go into the opposite classroom for Spanish. Instead of laughing at me, they helped me up, collected my books for me, and explained that that girl had always been a troublemaker. I'd already made an enemy? Presumably because I couldn't (and wouldn't if I could!) get her tickets to see my brother's band? Wonderful. (Word spread at the end of year nine that said girl was "encouraged" to leave before year ten rolled around, as she had caused a lot more trouble as time went on, not just with me but many others too. Whether that's entirely true or not, she wasn't there after summer was over, and year ten felt stress free!)

My first day at school was a bit unusual because it really *was* only a first for me. And as you can see, it didn't go all that well. The girl who tripped me up went on to cause all sorts of trouble for me over my first three years at high school, some of which I'll talk about later. But even knowing everything she had in store for me, I can still look back and take some positives from that day. Saffron, or Saffy as I now know her, went on to become one of my best friends, and six years after we left school we still meet up for coffee and a catch up every few months, along with our other good friend, Vicky. So even if you are the "new girl" (or boy!) and things aren't working out the way you hoped, remember to keep an eye out for friendly faces, and if they smile at you, smile back!

First days at school (or college!) are always going to be a bit nerve-wracking, especially if you don't know anyone at all beforehand. But the main thing to remember is that everyone else is just as nervous and just as eager to make friends, even if they have friends within the school already. No one wants to be disliked or make a prat out of themselves on their first day, so you're all in the same boat. All you really need to focus on is being nice to anyone who approaches you, asking for help or directions when you need it, and remembering that you're not the only one who's nervous!

Remember to keep an eye out for friendly faces, and smile back!

ROMANCE

Now this one is the biggie. Humans are hardwired to crave love, affection, and attention. As adults we learn how to deal with that craving a little better, how to suppress it and get on with life, but as teenagers, when hormones and intense feelings are only just kicking in, it can become overwhelming and all-consuming. I remember pining and longing for a certain boy when I was fourteen and it was *all* I could think about. I'd doodle hearts and soppy lyrics into my rough exercise book during class and my mind rarely wandered anywhere else!

So your best friend has got a boyfriend. You've heard some girl in your class has had her first kiss and is telling everyone about it. You've heard that some girl in the year above has had sex with her boyfriend of only ten days. One question:

So what?

That doesn't mean *you* should feel that you have to do anything, if you don't feel you're ready to. There is nothing you *should* be doing when it comes to romance and relationships. It's all personal choice and preference, so just because other people are experiencing these firsts before you, it doesn't mean there's an expiration date. Your romantic firsts are supposed to be (and yes, I am aware how cheesy this will sound) *special*. And they won't feel special if you're rushing them just because you want to catch up to everyone else. Those girls who are smooching, and, and . . . whatnot? Good for them. Whatever! They clearly feel that they are ready and that's their choice. But that doesn't mean you have to be too.

One of the main things to remember is that, following the First Kiss, First Boyfriend, and all the Firsts that seem desirable, will come the First Break-Up and the First Heartbreak. Not all firsts are fun, especially when you're younger and your emotions are on an all-time high. It won't be long before those friends you were so envious of start saying, "You had it right! Boys SUCK!" or, "I wish I hadn't shared my first kiss with him!" That's when you'll realize that it's not about how quickly you can experience everything, but about waiting for the right time.

When you finally *do* feel ready to experience certain romantic firsts . . . well, all in good time. I know it sounds clichéd, but stop looking for it and it'll find you. (I've stopped looking for Johnny Depp. He'll find me.) I can't tell you how true that is. I used to be in a desperate rush to have a boyfriend and feel loved and wanted and kissed, but as soon as I stopped being bothered and focused on something else, some-*one* else came along and swept me off my feet, happily ruining whatever it was I was previously focused on! It's only looking back now that I wish I hadn't been as bothered from the start and just let things play out. I wasted a lot of time, effort, and emotion wanting romance to make its grand entrance into my life when there were more important things I could have been focusing on. So, I know it's frustrating because all of your instincts are screaming, "I DON'T WANT TO BE FOREVER ALOOONNNEEEE! FIND ME SOMEONE QUICKLY!" But, trust me, the waiting is worth it when you find someone better suited and more special to you than those other someones you could have kissed simply because it meant not having to wait. I didn't have my first proper boy-friend until I was sixteen. A friend of mine didn't meet some-one she wanted to share anything with until she was nineteen. A male friend of mine is just in his first relationship at the age of twenty-two. Everyone is entirely different, and we all go through life at different speeds. It doesn't mean someone is doing it wrong or right. Just different, and that should be accepted and respected.

And, believe me, that first time you kiss someone who you're *really* into . . . it's explosive. Your skin is electric and you feel like your body has been set alight. Suddenly, you're so aware of everything, every touch, every move, every sound, and I've found either your mind races ten to the dozen or it turns to mush. It's different with different people of course, but when I've kissed people I've been seriously into it feels exactly like that. Then again, I've also kissed people who I haven't really been too fired up about following a series of weird events and it's . . . well, quite frankly it's boring, and you wonder why you wasted a kiss. If you treat your kisses like they're gold, as if you only have a limited supply of them, you'll only ever want to give them out to the people who you really trust with them and who you feel actually deserve them. I wish I'd been less liberal with my kisses as a teen. It's not like I snogged the face off every guy I ever met, but I did kiss a few people simply because they leaned in for one and I didn't know how to say no. Looking back, I wish I'd just gently pushed them away and let them down kindly, rather than giving away a precious kiss that I could have used on someone who I really wanted to share it with, someone who would make the hairs on the back of my neck stand on end and send me home with my lips turning up at the corners.

Kisses can be truly magical things that make you feel invincible and make two people sink into one for a brief moment, but on the flip side they can also be boring and awkward as hell when you're sharing them with someone who you're not sure of your feelings for. There's nothing worse than waiting for a kiss to end and then not knowing what to say once it has. It's not like you can say, "Hey, that was kind of dull because I don't actually really like you all that much. Let's not do that again!" So, please, I'm begging you, don't put yourselves through it—wait until you've found the right person before you rush into anything. Who's the right person? Someone you trust. Someone who you *like* like. Someone who trusts you too. Someone who *like* likes you too. How do you find those things out? USE YOUR WORDS. (More on this later.) Once you've found that person, your kisses and anything beyond will be like fireworks.

My Firsts

You've already heard about my first day at school, so let's move swiftly on to my first kiss. I'll admit, it was an odd one.

I certainly didn't wait for the right person. I was ten years old, in year six, and it was with a boy I'd fancied for ages but only because he read books and didn't mind sitting with me at lunch—something for which he was made fun of frequently. Lining our school playground was a giant hedge that foot-balls, tennis balls, and on one occasion my shoes got stuck in. On this particular day, it was the perfect hiding place to share a first kiss. It was sloppy, inexperienced, and just not what I expected, as a lot of first kisses are. As I'm sure you've guessed, I wish I'd waited.

My first day at my first job, in the West End show *Les Misérables,* was very different from my first day at school. No one had any idea who I was, or who I was related to, or what my previous jobs had been. It didn't really matter, and it con-tinued not to matter once they did know. We were older and more mature, and very aware that our main reason for having met in the first place was to get a job done—as we had very little time, it felt, to cram the whole score and blocking of a mammoth hit show into our brains! Meeting new people and making friends was a wonderful bonus that we got to enjoy while working on a beautiful, empowering show. But was I still nervous? Hell, yes. Was I still wondering what everyone thought of me when I walked into the room? Definitely. Was everyone else thinking exactly the same thing? After having spoken to them about our first day on the job a year down the line, yes. They were all as scared as I was, and that's built up my confidence for my next job after *Les Mis.* I'll be more sure that everyone else is just as nervous as I am, and I'm sure I'll have more courage to break the ice and say hello, being far more certain that others will accept that greeting with open arms.

The first day or the first time you do something is just the tiniest portion of that thing as a whole, and yet it's the bit we worry about and build up to the most. Once you get through the first day, you relax because it wasn't as hard or as nerve-wracking as you first thought it would be. Hindsight is beautifully annoying, is it not? But no matter how old you get, there will always be something you haven't experienced yet. I've still got so many memorable firsts to come. Hopefully by the time you're holding this book and reading it, I will have moved into my first flat (and started paying my first mortgage), paid my first bill, and had to learn how to do many things for the first time that my parents have always taken care of. And then after that in years to come I'll be getting married for the first (and hopefully last!) time, and after that I'll have my first child. Not to end this chapter on a jittery note, but there's always something you could get worked up about! It's all probably, fingers crossed, going to happen at some point, so instead of panicking you may as well sit back, relax, and let it happen.

TOP TIPS FOR DEALING
WITH STRESSFUL SITUATIONS

Blow on your thumb! This helps regulate your breathing a little better if you're nervous. This is particularly useful when you're about to go on stage and perform to a crowd—a tried-and-tested Carrie technique!

Talk about it! Talk to the people around you, or join in existing conversations and see how others feel about the situation.

Count to ten before you say anything! I tend to say things I regret later when I'm nervous. Counting to ten before I say things makes me think twice about what I want to say and whether it will make things worse or better.

Sleep on it! When I'm in a stressful situation, things tend to seem worse right before I go to bed. I don't really know why—I think it's because I've run out of time to solve the problem at hand and need to sleep, so it makes me feel more stressed out. However, as soon as I wake up the next morning I always feel so much better, and things seem far clearer when I have the whole day to put things right again!

2

Making Friends

I USED TO GET BULLIED WHEN I WAS IN PRIMARY SCHOOL. A lot. It
started off when my classmates noticed I had blonde hair and
brown eyes. A rare combo, I'll admit, but a very odd thing
to be bullied for. Then, when I started acting more and more
and had to take time away from school, I would find that
whenever I came back to class the friend groups had shifted.
I'd missed certain jokes that everyone shared as a class; I
didn't know that Pokémon cards were out and Yu-Gi-Oh
cards were in; I didn't own a BeyBlade yet, which was apparently the latest craze . . . I was like an alien to them and
they sure made me feel like one! "Shut up, Carrie!" became
something of a catchphrase. So, I sort of shrank away inside
myself. I became very shy and timid, and I wasn't so keen on
being myself if "being myself" meant having a chair thrown
at me across a classroom. (True story.) I learned that if I never
said anything, they couldn't tell me to shut up. So, moving
to a new high school, about twenty minutes' drive from my
primary school, had felt like a good move. All the kids from
my old school would be headed to the local high school and
certainly wouldn't be following me to this new place—or
"Hogwarts," as I liked to call it. It was so far removed from

anything I'd ever known, it might as well have been a school in a castle for magical children in a place you could only reach by a train on a hidden platform! But, as I've already explained, walking into that Hogwarts classroom for the first time after two months away, missing everything that I'd missed, made me feel like that alien all over again. Once the trauma of that first day was over, however, I resolved to shush my Inner Critic and said, "No. This *will not* be the same as last time. I won't be that shy, downtrodden little girl any more. It's time to actually make some friends."

I didn't want to have to squish down my personality any-more, and surely now that I was at a new school I had no reason to? Sure, I had some boundaries to overcome, and I needed to prove I wasn't that snobby, stagey theater girl they all thought I was, but that didn't mean I had to pretend I was someone else or not be myself to the fullest.

But how? How does someone who's lacking in social confidence and any skills in making friends actually end up talking to people they'll call friends for life? Well, guys, here are some of my top tips for making friends in all situations, be it at school, college, work, or any general scenario where you could potentially meet a BFF.

1. BEING YOURSELF

This is my first and most important tip for meeting and mak-ing new friends, because the person you introduce yourself as influences how people perceive you and the sort of people you attract! In my head, I went through a million different types of "me" I could be before my first day at high school. Would I be the moody and mysterious type? Loud and bubbly? Odd and quirky? Shy and timid? Extremely girly? Tomboyish?

Who was it that I *wanted* to be? In the end I could[n't make] up my mind, so to begin with I tried to exaggerate c[ertain] aspects of my personality with different types of people.

Sporty   EMO   Girly

I soon realized I had a few friends here and there in lots of different cliques, but I didn't really have any close friends who knew everything about me. No one knew who I really was in my entirety. This made me quite sad, and I started to drop the acts. It had become an effort playing up my tomboyish side with the sporty crowd when we were playing rounders. It was hard work emphasizing my girly streak when the girls started talking about TV shows I didn't really like. I was a little bit tomboyish, what with having grown up with a brother to guide me through life up until then, but that didn't define me. That wasn't the be all and end all of my personality. And I did like clothes and doing my hair, but I didn't wear make-up or like shopping unless it was for books! I was trying to be who everyone else expected me to be to fit in with *everyone*, forgetting that people aren't designed to be

I don't have to be everyone's friend; nor ... pecially when it's not actually *me* being

... pretend to like and dislike things just ... at's the expected answer. Be honest ... and feel, and those who also think and ... the same way will gravitate toward you.

2. APPROACHING PEOPLE

Actually walking up to someone and introducing yourself, for me, is the most daunting part of making friends. Sometimes you watch people from afar that you'd just love to be friends with, but you feel that just walking up to them and saying hello would do more damage than good! They might think you're weird or dorky. So, how do you actually start talking to them?

Personally, I learned to just suck it up and do it. The simplest and easiest way to speak to someone is . . . to speak to them! It takes a lot of tries to build up the confidence to be able to do it naturally, and it may seem awkward and uncomfortable at first, but it's important to persevere and push past it. I've built up so much courage doing it over the years that I literally walked up to someone on a train platform the other day to tell her that her hair, which was dyed all different colors, was freaking awesome. She looked very pleased! The more practice you get at talking to people, the better you become, but of course taking that first step is rather scary.

Why not open with a question? Think of a band you like and ask if they like them too. If they're wearing something you think is cool, ask them where they got it. Is there a TV show you watched last night that you really enjoyed? Ask them if they watched it too. Breaking the ice is the hardest bit, but if you open with a question, it puts the ball in their court and it's up to them to respond.

3. A LITTLE BIT OF STALKING

OK, I don't mean proper full-on sitting-across-the-road-hidden-in-some-bushes-wearing-camouflage-with-binoculars-and-a-box-of-jam-donuts kind of stalking. I mean a little bit of light and harmless social-media stalking. (I'll talk about my beef with the term "stalking" when it comes to social media a little later, but, for now, I'll use it to get my point across.) If you send someone a friend request and they've accepted, you're already halfway there. They've allowed you access to all their holiday snaps, pictures of pets, and unnecessary status updates about what they have for breakfast, lunch, and dinner. If that's not friendship, then I don't know what is! But seriously, from their profiles on Facebook, Twitter, and Tumblr, you'll get a general idea of what they're into, their likes and dislikes, and whether you think you would get along. Once you've got a few things you can relate to them with, work on step number two and approach them in a friendly way about something they're interested in!

4. A REASON TO LIKE THE INTERNET

While we're on it, I still maintain that speaking to someone IRL is the best way to befriend them, but if you have real issues with it and you fear you may pass out and/or vomit on their shoes if you do, why not strike up a conversation from behind the safety of your computer screen? When you get to the Internet section of this book, you'll see why this may be one of the only scenarios in which I'll encourage speaking to someone textually via a computer screen rather than speaking to them face to face. But, hey, if that's what works for you and helps you make friends and eventually find the bravery to speak to someone in person, so be it. Go for it!

Making friends doesn't necessarily have to be difficult or daunting. Most of the time it just sort of happens without us even realizing. You sit next to someone in class/in the office/on the bus for a week or two, and saying hello every morning develops into a chat, which develops into coffee, which develops into a standing coffee date every couple of weeks. Sometimes it happens as naturally as that. Sometimes it doesn't, and we watch those people we'd love to be friends with from afar, just wishing we could know what their voice sounds like saying, "You're my best friend, Carrie!" It's sad when someone you want to be friends with doesn't reciprocate, for whatever reason. But we can't be friends with everyone—some sociologists have suggested that the average adult has two genuinely close

> **Really special, worth-moving-the-earth-for friends are hard to find.**

friends, and that's because really special, worth-moving-the-earth-for friends are hard to find, and close friendships take commitment and hard work. So don't beat yourself up about the number of friends you have, or if you just don't click with a new acquaintance. But likewise, don't let the fear of rejection put you off making the effort. All it takes is a little courage to take that first step. From then on it's up to the *both* of you to make it happen!

3

Work Versus Play

IN MY *EARLY* DAYS OF HIGH SCHOOL, I was the biggest pair of goody two shoes there ever was. I was like those massive '80s platform shoes that make you ten feet tall . . . except, being a goody two shoes, I would never have been caught dead in platform shoes like that, as they weren't school regulation. Flat, black patent shoes for me. The same as my Latin teacher in fact . . . you can imagine how that went down when my friends figured that out. I wasn't a goody two shoes in the sense that I knew all the answers to every question ever asked or that I gave an apple to all my teachers every day. Just in the sense that I never wanted to intentionally do anything that could potentially get me into any trouble—to the point where it stopped me from having any kind of fun. You wouldn't have been able to find anyone else who followed the rule book as meticulously as I did when I first joined my high school. My homework was done the night of the day it had been handed out, I was early for every lesson, and you never saw me wearing nail polish or dangly earrings like some of the other girls (for fear of ending up in detention like a lot of them did). I was a real-life Hermione Granger. Far less clever, of course, but, much like Hermione, I became far more relaxed and a little more mischievous as time went on!

I was in year eight or nine, I think, and it was the last day of term and the last day of school for the year elevens. They were planning *something*—I didn't know what exactly, but I knew it would be pretty huge, a proper send-off. For some reason, the little devil on my shoulder possessed me; I was dying to be a part of it, and I knew two girls in that year who were happy to involve me in their plans.

"You can be our lookout," they said, and I eagerly agreed. This little ball of nervous energy formed halfway between my chest and my stomach as soon as I'd said yes. An energy telling me that I was going to get into trouble but simultaneously telling me not to care. I vowed to myself, if things started to go arse over teakettle then I'd back out and that was that.

On the day, the school was mayhem. The hallways had been covered in confetti made of chopped-up school paperwork, the door handles had been freshly Vaselined, and every classroom had been given a little bowl filled with a few centimeters of water and a goldfish swimming circles around the bottom. As I recall, our class goldfish was called Gremlin. The day went by, everyone tense, expecting the next eruption of trickery around every corner, but by the end of lunchtime, things had died down. I thought they had, at least. Ten minutes before classes started again, one of the girls came to collect me in preparation for whatever it was they had planned. I was given strict instructions that if I saw the head of sixth form, Mr. Elliott, come out of the staffroom and head their way, I had to stall him or run ahead and let the girls know he was on the prowl. I was quite literally buzzing, hopping from foot to foot in nervous excitement, half of me dreading Mr. Elliott walking through those doors and half of me wanting him to, to give me a purpose. Each time that staffroom door opened, I was almost a little bit sick in my mouth, on the brink of a nervous breakdown. Suddenly, I heard a clatter, a scramble, and scattered giggles above me, so I turned around to watch the prank of all pranks arise in all its glory. There on the roof of the cafeteria, slowly inflating or, err . . . should I say, erecting, was a six-foot inflatable penis with a group of girls standing around it, proudly cheering as loud as they could. The prank was well and truly a success. You had to appreciate the amount of effort they'd put into a trick that lasted all of five minutes! I doubled over and laughed into the stone paving for a solid few minutes, and when I arose again Mr. Elliott, the head of sixth form himself, was standing next to me. But he didn't look angry.

"Come on, girls." He broke off to stifle a giggle. "Prank's over, very good." Mr. Elliott sent me back to class with nothing but a roll of his eyes, and I went on my way knowing I'd witnessed something pretty awesome and undeniably something I'd remember for a long time to come.

For me, that was quite a pivotal moment. I had overworked myself and never allowed myself any time to just chill out. From then on out, I realized I still could get my work done but spend my free time having fun with my friends and doing what I wanted to do. I think that's why I eventually came to enjoy school so much. To this day, I'm the only one out of my friends who still misses it! I miss my school days with every fiber of my being because I made sure I made the most of them.

I was never involved in anything else as dramatic as the penis incident, or anything that could have landed me in *serious* trouble, but I discovered a naughty streak lying right under the surface of the exterior my teachers had already deemed "angelic." I played mild pranks like flicking ink from my cartridge pens at friends when they weren't looking, or doing my hair up in mad ways and insisting to my math teacher that this was how everyone was wearing it these days, and sometimes I'd even hum one note quietly in a silent class to see how long it took before someone noticed and identified me as the source—which they never did!

I'm not saying you should all smuggle inflatable genitalia onto your school roofs or anything to that extreme, nor am I telling everyone to play pranks instead of doing homework! It's all about finding that balance between the two. If you focus on schoolwork to the exclusion of all else, you'll get past your final exams, look back, and wonder why you spent your school years only ever seeing the inside of a textbook. But likewise, if it's all pranks and no work, you may not even get past those final exams!

RIP, Mr Elliott

4

Asking Questions

WHEN I WAS IN MY EARLY YEARS AT HIGH SCHOOL, years seven to
nine I'd say, I hated drawing attention to myself (says the
actress). I didn't like putting my hand up to answer questions, even if I knew the right answer, and I especially didn't
like asking for help if I didn't understand something or if I
needed something to be repeated. I was also that girl who
was prone to quietly nattering with mates during class, drawing in my notebooks, writing lyrics and poems, and basically
doing anything I possibly could to make the time go faster
in lessons such as math, biology, and Spanish which, unfortunately, meant I *needed* things to be repeated from time to
time. I'd always nudge my friends and whisper, "Ask her for
me! Ask her!" so that I didn't have to put myself in the firing
line in case the teacher accused me of not listening, which, of
course, was unbelievably unfair on my friends!

One day, one of my friends asked *me* to ask our teacher
something for her, and for some reason I was feeling cou-
rageous and went for it. I was polite and apologetic that "I"
hadn't heard, and my teacher happily repeated the homework
assignment. After class, a bunch of my friends came to me
and said thank God I'd asked that question because they also

hadn't heard, or had forgotten by the time they'd gotten to writing it down, and they were too scared to ask themselves. What on earth would we have done if no one had plucked up the courage to ask? We all would have left the room not having a clue what homework we were doing and would have been in far more trouble in our next lesson when we had nothing to give our teacher. Sometimes asking questions doesn't just help you out, but the people around you too. If you've not been listening, it is your own fault so make sure it's YOU that asks for a repetition rather than pushing your friends ahead of you. You'd feel awful if they got told off in your place, wouldn't you?

Not listening is one thing. Not *understanding* is another. Your teachers may seem grouchy and scary at times, but it is their job to help you get through school and pass your exams. If you don't understand, ask them (or wait until after class and ask a friend who does), but do *not* keep quiet and hope the knowledge comes to you during the night like a bolt of lightning! Learning doesn't quite work like that. No one is good at everything, and sometimes we need a little bit of extra help when we feel like we're lagging behind. I was AWFUL at math. I mean just seriously horrendous. I spent my lessons trying so hard to understand, but ended up giving up and slapping my friend's head with my ruler. (One time I did that and it shattered against her head. We almost peed ourselves laughing.) However, my form tutor was also the math teacher of another group—he was a lovely, kind-natured man from New Zealand who was always willing to help and would also make lessons fun. So, in my lunchtimes I'd knock on the staffroom door and ask for his help. He'd think it was amusing to put things we liked into the equation. For me, it was cake. "So if you have *n* cakes and it's three to the power of *n* . . ." That kind of thing! (By the way, I have NO idea if that is even an equation or a math type . . . thing.)

There was a girl in a different English group than mine who was always getting ribbed by her friends for asking what they thought were stupid questions. Most notoriously, "How do you spell W?" (She was expecting it to be spelled out like "double you," totally forgetting that it's a letter, not a word!) She always took the jibes well and laughed it off, but, you've got to hand it to her, the girl had the courage to ask questions about things she just didn't understand! She may have been laughed at, but she ended up better off because she *learned*.

Asking questions can be difficult sometimes, especially when you feel that you're the only one not getting it and falling behind the group's pace, but it'll be worth it in the end when you're passing exams with flying colors and getting jobs done more efficiently.

5

Making Mistakes

AS MUCH AS WE MIGHT HATE TO ADMIT IT, WE ALL MAKE MISTAKES.
Some bigger than others, but no one can escape the wrath of
the mistake. What we forget is that we're *allowed* to make
them. It's just advisable not to make the same mistakes *again
and again*. That's when it becomes a conscious bad habit.

I've made a lot of mistakes. Most have been little hiccups
that I could easily correct with an apology, but some have
been whales of mistakes that needed profuse apologies (verbal
and written) and proof that it would never, not in my lifetime,
ever, EVER happen again.

I once received a message asking me how you forget a
mistake and move on from it. I thought about it for a while,
looking back at all the mistakes I'd made that still make
me feel like absolute crap, and I realized that I'm *glad* I still
remember them after all this time, because they're a reminder
of what not to do to create an awkward situation, what not to
say to piss off my mum, what I shouldn't have done instead
of doing my coursework, and so on and so forth. Once
you've made that mistake, and assuming you're the sort of
person who realizes what a stupid thing it was to do—to the

extent that you know years later you'll *still* feel terrible that you did it—you'll know not to make the same mistake for a second time.

When we make mistakes on our homework, it's easy to correct. All it takes is a bit of Wite-Out, some scribbling out, or a new page. Mistakes in life are harder to correct, and sometimes they're also harder to admit to. Whenever I made mistakes in science, it was me versus cold, hard factual answers. It was very easy for me to say, "Yes, I am wrong. Nemo wouldn't actually have been able to talk in real life." But when it's a case of feelings and opinions, it's so much harder to tell who's wrong, who's right, and who should be apologizing.

When I was at school, my friends and I would bicker about silly things every now and then, as you do when you spend every day with the same people. We'd catch each other in bad moods, or become a little careless with what we said or how we acted, and it resulted in stints of the cold shoulder or a lunchtime row. Friendships are difficult things because of course you still respect and love your friends even when you argue, but it's hard not to *also* feel like you want to punch them in the face a little bit. (Just me? Oh . . . !)

It's so easy to find yourselves arguing in circles because neither of you wants to be the one to admit that, if you'd done something just a little bit differently, you wouldn't be arguing.

Me: If you'd just done that, we could have avoided this!

Friend: Sure, but if YOU'D just done THIS, we wouldn't be having this conversation either!

The argument just goes on and on until you run out of things to say or until one of you has to leave the room! I found myself in that situation over and over again at school, and it never felt any easier to admit that maybe I was the one in the irritable mood, or maybe I actually kind of knew my friend didn't mean what she said in that way, and yes, my friend could have handled it better but . . . so could I!

Holding up your hands and saying, "It was my fault, I'm sorry," is incredibly hard. There's nothing worse than getting halfway through an argument and realizing, actually, maybe, sort of, you are a little bit in the wrong, but you wouldn't believe how much easier it ultimately makes the whole situation if you just say that, there and then. Obviously, don't say it just to end an argument you're bored of, or to try to look like "the bigger person"; do it because you've genuinely realized it's your fault. It becomes very clear when you realize you're wrong and you're arguing just because you can't admit that it's you who has made a mistake. But I tell you what, people will really respect you for being brave enough to do it.

Also, you can avoid getting into situations like that. If you're one hundred percent sure that you're right but someone challenges you, politely say that you're "pretty sure." If it turns out that you are in fact right, it makes it easier for the other person to admit it was their mistake, and you don't look like a smug, arrogant winner who's dying to say "I told you so!" However, if you're anything less than one hundred percent sure, you could say something like, "I'm not entirely certain but . . ." and then if you *are* wrong, you've safeguarded yourself and it'll be easier for you to say "Oh, you were right!" Don't go in all guns blazing, claiming that your knowledge is the right knowledge when you're actually not that certain. Even if you *are* one hundred percent certain, no one likes a know-it-all!

Making mistakes makes us all feel a bit stupid, and it's not something that can be avoided. *To err is human.* It's how you *handle* the mistake that defines you, so work on saying "It's my fault" because lord knows you'll need to do that from time to time in your life. But also, don't be afraid to make mistakes in the first place! That's how we learn. Never do anything half-heartedly just because you're afraid something may go slightly wrong. Something is *always* bound to go slightly wrong somewhere, so you might as well just go for it. No one who is anyone got anywhere by thinking, *But what if I screw up?!* In the words of Madame Leota in the film *The Haunted Mansion* (the film adaptation of what happens to be my favorite Disney World ride . . .), "You try, you fail, you try, you fail, but the only true failure is when you stop trying." And mistakes are sometimes blessings in disguise. Alexander Fleming sure as hell wasn't trying to create penicillin during his experiments, but look how many lives that mistake has saved! You learn *so* much from going wrong, so don't be afraid to. Embrace the wrongness, because it'll make the eventual rightness even sweeter!

> Don't be afraid to make mistakes in the first place! That's how we learn.

6

How To Apologize

AS WE LEARNED FROM THE LAST CHAPTER, no one likes to admit they're wrong. Myself included. I hate that sinking feeling I get when I realize that maybe I'm actually kinda, sorta, OK a helluva lot wrong, or maybe I've made a mistake and need to own up and say sorry. No matter what situation you're in, it takes guts to say, "You know, I am wrong and I'm extremely sorry." But d'ya know what? It makes *so* much difference to a relationship when you can say sorry and not have it be a big deal. No "I told you so" and no "I'm *always* right." Just "sorry," and "I accept your apology," and a healthier friendship for it.

I used to be so rubbish at saying sorry. Although of course it's not the *saying* sorry that's hard, it's the admitting that you have something to say you're sorry *for*. I'd do everything I could to make sure I wasn't the one that had to say it. Until, one day, something clicked in my brain. If I was in a situation where someone else was wrong and they apologized to me as soon as they realized their mistake, I'd respect them so much more for apologizing without fighting, which would have prolonged an unpleasant situation for us both. The important thing when you find yourself arguing with someone you're friends with or someone you love (which is inevitable, I'm afraid!) isn't *winning* the argument. It's *ending* the argument without having done lasting damage to your relationship. If you already know you're wrong but won't admit it and say sorry, that could potentially make things worse not just in the short term, but for the future too.

So, here are a few tips for apologizing and accepting those apologies!

1. IF YOU KNOW YOU'RE WRONG, SAY YOU'RE WRONG

What do you think is going to happen if you don't admit that you've realized you're wrong? That they'll never find out? And is that a risk you want to take? If it's a case of arguing over a fact, they can just Google the hell out of it as soon as you part ways and realize you were wrong on their own. That's going to make things extremely awkward for you when they confront you with actual factual evidence and there's no way you can deny it. If it's something where the lines between right and wrong are a little more blurred, why blur them further by refusing to admit you've realized that you're the one in the wrong? When a situation has lots of intricate ins and outs, the damage an argument can do can last a good long while, so if you

> The important thing is *ending* the argument without having done lasting damage to your relationship.

have that sudden realization halfway through that maybe you're the one to blame, just hold your hands up and accept that blame with open arms before the situation gets worse. The important thing is that you're not arguing anymore and the situation has been resolved. Not who was right and who was wrong.

2. EVEN IF IT WAS UNINTENTIONAL, YOU STILL HAVE TO SAY YOU'RE SORRY

A lot of people think that if you didn't *mean* to hurt someone's feelings, you don't have to say you're sorry. I'm afraid to say that if you think that, you're a bit of a twonk! Someone's feelings are still hurt *because of you*. Think of it like this: I'm sitting next to you in the cinema and as I get up to go to the toilet I tread on your toe. (OK, I'll be honest, I'm going to get a family-size bag of Minstrels that, let's face it, I'm not going to share . . .) I'm not going to refuse to apologize because I wasn't intentionally trying to stamp on your foot. Your foot still hurts, doesn't it? Because *my* foot crushed it under all ten stone nine pounds of *my* weight, right? So, even though my intentions were good, and all I wanted was a bag of Minstrels, the blame is still mine to bear and apologize for.

The same goes for feelings. If you didn't mean to hurt someone's feelings but you've still managed to hurt them, then for goodness' sake, apologize for it! Sometimes we say things or do things that we think are completely innocent— and often they are entirely that—but inadvertently upset someone because of that thing we said or did. It doesn't matter that our main goal was something a million miles away from upsetting that person, unfortunately we still managed to do so, and we need to say sorry for it.

I've known a few people who couldn't grasp that concept, and the fact they would rather stand by what they said and ignore the hurt feelings of someone they care about, rather than own up to the mistake they made, always upset me far more than whatever it was they said or did in the first place.

3. INTENTIONS STILL MATTER

Even though good intentions don't get you out of saying sorry, it does make a difference to someone if you weren't *trying* to hurt their feelings. Well, it does to me anyway. A friend of mine once made a joke at my expense in which he implied I was, well . . . "easy." It upset me, of course, but he's my friend, and I know that he didn't intend to upset me and never thought it would annoy me as much as it did. He explained that, had he known how much it would upset me, he never would have said it and apologized for doing so. That meant a lot to me, and I forgave him far more quickly for his stupid joke than if he'd said it to intentionally push my buttons. It's the difference between a friend and a bit of a meanie! Just something to think about the next time your friend apologizes and explains their good intentions.

4. DON'T MAKE EXCUSES BUT DO EXPLAIN

The difference between an excuse and an explanation is that an excuse is designed to get you out of apologizing. An explanation usually comes *with* an apology. For instance, "the dog ate my homework" is a classic example of an excuse that tries to get someone off the hook because they're placing all the blame on the poor dog's shoulders. Whereas if someone explained that they don't have their homework because their dog ate it, but it was their fault for not keeping an eye on the homework (and the dog), that's a perfect explanation of the situation they've gotten themselves into, while still acknowledging that it's something *they've* done. Giving context for *why* you ended up hurting someone is hugely important for (a) the person you've upset to understand better exactly why they're upset and (b) the person who did the upsetting to understand how they can avoid doing the same thing in the future. If you start to hear yourself explaining why you don't feel like you're to blame, you're making an excuse to show the other person why it's not your fault, rather than apologizing for the fact you've upset someone. Give context for your actions for everyone's better understanding of the situation, but still apologize.

5. DON'T SAY "I TOLD YOU SO"

Nothing is less attractive than an insufferable know-it-all, and it really makes apologizing a lot harder for the other person when you make a big fuss out of being right. We all know how hard it is to admit to a mistake, so imagine how hurtful it is when a friend finally plucks up the courage to confess that maybe they were wrong and then you (metaphorically) strip off to your underwear, start happy dancing, and yell, "I KNEW IT! YOU'RE WRONG, I'M RIGHT! I TOLD YOU SO! NER NER NER NER NER!!!" That would suck. Don't do that. Realize just how difficult it was to say "I'm wrong, I'm sorry," accept that apology, and just be thankful that you're no longer arguing with someone you like and spend enough time with to get into an argument in the first place!

Admitting that we're wrong is one thing, but apologizing for being wrong is even harder.

THE SAR-CHASM

Some say sarcasm is the lowest form of wit. Some scientific studies say that it's been proven to make you cleverer. I'm no scientist or linguistic expert, but I know from experience when NOT to be sarcastic, and it's when you're in an argument.

In the heat of a row, I often find myself being extreme. My sarcasm goes off the scale (if there was one—the sarky-o-meter!).

> *Oh, why don't you both just get married!*

> *Oh wonderful! That's JUST what I needed to hear!*

> *What a brilliant thing to say, YOU GENIUS!*

Have you ever had that feeling of knowing what you just said made everything go from bad to "Holy crap!" in 0.6 seconds? That the words that just wafted from your lips have polluted the air between you and the poor recipient forever? It creates a chasm between you . . .

Within relationships especially, sarcasm was always my defense mechanism as soon as things got heated. I've got this awful affliction where my tear ducts are triggered by anger. As soon as I get frustrated in the heat of a row I start crying and I'm unable to talk any more; therefore anything I do manage to say is written off as the ravings of a hysterical weeping mess and I'm no longer taken seriously. I eventually figured out that if I kept a hard (and slightly aggressive) exterior, I could voice my problems without getting emotional, and sarcasm allowed me to do this perfectly. Sarcasm usually involves taking an extreme position to make a point, and that's often the worst thing you can do in an argument because it blows everything out of proportion or, as they say, "makes a mountain out of a mole hill."

I'm far from perfect, but the worst versions of even the best people can be pretty damn awful sometimes, and it's just part of being human to feel the heat and rage of an argument. We all get like that from time to time, but I've learned that things end up so much better and have a better bearing on the future when arguments don't get vicious.

Usually, we use sarcasm when someone is hurting or annoying us. We say what it is that they're doing, sarcastically, as if it's not hurting us at all.

"Of COURSE that last piece of cake was for you. That's why it was at the back of the fridge with a Post-It note stuck to its plate with MY name on it!"

(A light-hearted example, of course. Although cake is a very serious matter to me . . .)

It's entirely fine to voice our problems to the people causing them, because communication is one of the best, yet underused, ways to solve problems . . . but only if you're saying something that calms the situation rather than inflames it. So, here are my top tips for arguments that may or may not help you . . . but they sure helped me!

- I try to keep a calm tone, even if I'm fired up.
- I try to Use My Words. Aha, here's where we get to it. Use your words. Saying "Right now I feel [insert emotion] because [insert reason]" is far more effective than hiding what you feel only for it to bubble to the surface again later. There is never any need to be mean or inappropriate, but it's so much better for everyone involved if you calmly and tactfully just say exactly how you feel and why you feel that way. It gets to the heart of the problem sooner, and it creates a far more open and honest relationship.

Don't use sarcasm to be mean or for impact. It will only chip away at the foundations of your relationship, and it doesn't just go away once the argument is over. Often the things people say during rows stick around only to be brought up and over-analyzed later. So, try to take the thing that is bothering you that you would usually say sarcastically ("Oh, what a brilliant idea it is leaving your shoes in the middle of the floor exactly where everyone can trip over them! You genius!") and turn it into a calm suggestion about how you can move forward ("It really frustrates me when you leave your shoes in the middle of the floor and I have to pick them up. Could you make an effort not to do that anymore?"). (Although, if that is what's bothering you, take a look at the chapter "Does It Really Matter?")

Sometimes, a little bit of sarcasm—if used with the intention of making someone smile during a silly fight—can tip you both into a fit of giggles, during which the argument dissipates. But if it's used during an argument that's a little more serious, even if the intent is still the same, it could make the other person far more angry because it seems like you're not taking the situation as seriously as they are. Oof, it's all so complicated and confusing, isn't it?

We all get riled up and heated and we all end up saying things we don't mean. My sarcasm has been the nail in the coffin of relationships before. Luckily, I've learned from my mistakes, and I'm doing far better at avoiding sar-chasms now. Instead of being intentionally mean or trying to hit a nerve, it's best to try and deal with things peacefully while still voicing whatever it is that's bothering you. It brings it to the other person's attention and after that you've just got to hope they respond positively!

ACT 2

Not Everyone Is Going to Like You . . . and Why That Doesn't Matter!

7

Hindsight

I WAS RECENTLY HAVING COFFEE WITH A GOOD FRIEND OF MINE, Alan Cole. He's one of my dearest friends, and I clicked with him as soon as we met. (A quick aside about the first time we met: I was nineteen, at a party on a rooftop in Soho, London. I confessed to him I'd only been drunk once and never enough to spew.* He then made it his aim to get me as drunk as possible . . . and that night was one of my firsts. Not one I'm proud of, but it was a first all the same and hasn't been repeated since! Despite his questionable behavior, he did make sure I got home safely and text the next morning to make sure I was all right. Since that night of giggling, wonderful storytelling, and *far* too many tequila slushies, I've held a very special place for him in my heart.) Alan's like a puppy I feel I need to look after and, more often than not, he's happy to be looked after. We don't see each other often, but when we do it's always my favorite day of the week.

Anyway, on this particular occasion, we'd met for coffee and we were talking about our high school years. It turned out we

---

* In the UK, it's legal to drink at age 18. Don't get the wrong idea, USA readers!

both had a bit of a knack for being a little mischievous—he often got caught for his outlandish, well-planned school pranks and you already know about one of my more infamous escapades!

As we were chatting Alan told me about a friend of his who claimed to have had a "nemesis" at school.

"I wish I'd had a nemesis," he said longingly. "It sounds so epic!"

As I have previously mentioned, I made an enemy on my first day at school, and this wasn't a Cinderella deal; it didn't just last until midnight. Oh no, it went on for the next three years until she left. From the moment I denied her the McFly tickets, I was her favorite target. Looking back now, everything she said or did seems insignificant and rather petty and those memories no longer provoke the same feelings in me, but I can remember all too well how it made me feel back then. Every day, when I walked through those school gates, knowing she'd be there, I had a knot in my stomach that kept tightening, pulling me in toward it, forcing me to shrink into myself, and making me feel three feet smaller than everyone else. I felt sick every time I saw her walk into the classroom, knowing something was probably going to be said about the way I had my hair that day or the book I was reading would be hurled across the room because "reading was for nerds." I started to shuffle into school as only half of who I was because I couldn't grow when there was someone constantly cutting me down. (Like that line in *Pocahontas*: "How high does the sycamore grow? If you cut it down, then you'll never know.") I didn't want to be treated the same way as I was in primary school. I didn't want to be any less of myself now that I'd made friends I could be entirely "me" around. I didn't want to be a shell of a girl again. Back then, I had even less of a confrontational nature than I do now (and even now I can't order my own food in restaurants or pick up the phone to people I don't know!) so instead of thinking about what it would be like to poison her school lunch or pull her teeth out one by one, I was left thinking, *What did I do?* From my first day, until she left the school, I felt unnecessarily nervous and somewhat inadequate compared to the rest of my class-mates. She wasn't picking on *them*. What was it about me, specifically, that made someone treat me this way? What was I doing wrong to be made to feel this small? Did I do or say something specific? Was it just me as a person?

That little sod I mentioned earlier called *hindsight* allows me to see what was really going on more clearly, and now, looking back at myself and my "nemesis," I can plainly see . . .

It wasn't me.

Everyone has insecurities. Some are small and easy to ignore on a daily basis, and we only think about them when someone else points them out, but some are bigger and dom-inate everything. Some are things we constantly think and worry about—they are in the back of our minds, day in and day out. For instance, one of my biggest insecurities is a phys-ical thing. I have a little lump on my right forearm which is actually a scar from when my friend's parrot bit me (my life is ridiculous). It scarred because I'm an idiot and I kept picking the scab. It's been there for about six years now and, to be honest, it looks a bit gross and out of place. I've learned to live with it, but I went through a phase of constantly wearing a Band-Aid over it in case other people saw it and asked what it was. In actual fact, all the Band-Aid did was attract more attention to it and cause everyone to ask why I had a Band-

THE AMAZING GOGGLES OF HINDSIGHT

Aid there! I'm over the worst of the insecurity and, for the most part, I've accepted that the scar is there to stay—but the point is that everyone has a thing like that, something that they're always conscious of, whether it's physical, mental, or emotional. Some people deal with it well and even get over it. They work on or accept the thing that bothers them and turn it into an asset, something to be proud of. Or they talk to other people and discover that they also share the same insecurity, which makes them feel less alone.

However, some people deal with their little insecurities by picking on other people's. In other words, they become bullies. They think that drawing attention to the things they perceive to be wrong with *other* people draws attention away from what they think is wrong with themselves. It's the equivalent of someone pointing to nothing in the distance and shouting, "QUICK! LOOK! AN ELEPHANT!" in the hope that everyone looks at the elephant and ignores whatever it is they're trying to hide. It has absolutely nothing to do with the person they're attacking. They probably don't mean half the things they say and have more than likely made up the other half! The problem lies with the attacker, not the victim. And it's always worth remembering that sometimes the thing that they say is "wrong" with you is really something they're resentful or envious of. Perhaps a talent you have, or your obvious beauty, or that you're good at speaking in public.

The next time a bully picks on you for something you feel insecure about, take comfort in knowing that behind that insult is a swarm of their own insecurities buzzing around their heads, and they're trying to draw your attention away from whatever those things are. Feel sorry for them because they have far more problems than you do. Think about it. At what point do your own insecurities become so loud that you need to drown them out by actively being mean to the people around you? If only the bullies let those insecurities *out* and talked about them, they'd probably find that other people share them and it's not something that they need to feel insecure about in the first place.

I'm hoping that anyone reading this who is being bullied or is witnessing bullying can take this information, apply it, and share it. It's not an action you take or something you say. It's more a way of thinking. A different perspective on a sad situation that makes it a bit brighter, lighter, and easier to deal with. It's information that I learned too late, so instead of you guys getting five years down the line and thinking, *Oh!* That's *what that was. I wish I knew that then! I wouldn't have worried so much!* I'm giving you the power of hindsight when it's not . . . hind. Present-sight. Yeah. That's a thing now. Present-sight. *nods*

After I explained this to my dear friend Alan, he agreed that maybe having a nemesis or, in other words, your own personal bully, isn't nearly all it's cracked up to be. It's not like it appears in the movies—an

> A different perspective can make a sad situation a bit lighter, brighter, and easier to deal with.

epic battle of wits between two people, full of well-placed insults where people yell "BUUURRRNNNN!" afterwards; there are no seemingly awesome pranks involving half the school, a tub of bubbly detergent, a reel of copper wire, and three ducks, and in my case, there was certainly no happy ending where we all kissed and made up. In reality, although I enjoyed my school overall, that knot in my stomach every time I crossed the blue school gates is a feeling I may forgive but will never forget.

JEALOUSY

Over the last few years, I've become extremely inquisitive. I can't tell whether it's my mind asking more questions or whether it's always been that way and I just have more confidence to speak out and actually ask them out loud. As I've said before, when I was at school and I didn't understand something, I'd wait until someone else asked the same question or I'd quietly nudge my friends and make them ask for me. I was in fear of being laughed at for asking what a word meant or asking for a repetition of something I didn't quite catch the first time. What I realize now is that when I ask questions, I'm doing a favor to all the people around me who used to feel like me, desperately wanting to know the answers without the courage to ask. Of course, with Google at our disposal it's much easier to discreetly look things up, even when we're on the go. I must admit I have been known to whip my phone out under the table when someone uses a word like "superfluous" or "supercilious" . . . or any other "super" you can think of!

Not so long ago, through my verbal enquiries or my tap-tap-tapping on the Google machine, I discovered the difference between "jealousy" and "envy." "There's a difference?!" I hear you cry.

> *noun:* **jealousy**; *plural noun:* **jealousies**
> *Feeling or showing a resentful suspicion that one's partner is attracted to or involved with someone else.*

Jealousy is the word I find we use most often. It crops up in situations where you feel slightly peeved that someone else has got tickets to see your favorite band and you can't afford one, or when the boy/girl you like is looking at a different boy/girl. In actual fact, those two scenarios require two different words. So, I believe it's really envy that is the more common emotion.

> *noun:* **envy**; *plural noun:* **envies**
> *A feeling of discontented or resentful longing aroused by someone else's possessions, qualities, or luck.*

To *envy* is to bear a grudge against someone for possessing something you would like to own. You like them less for enjoying something that you can't have. It's a rather sordid emotion, albeit one we can't control—and what I mean is that we can't control those feelings arising, but we can definitely have a say in how we deal with them! So, *jealousy* is the word we use, but I think *envy* is the emotion we most commonly feel. The reason I think the two emotions are so often confused is because of romance. Of course. For instance, if I had a boyfriend who had a very close friendship with another girl, I would be *jealous* of my boyfriend's friendship with her, but I would be *envious* of the girl because of the affection she gets from my boyfriend. See where the wires have been crossed?

The reason I bring this up is because I've often had the phrase "they're just jealous!" thrown at me when someone's said something mean, and I am absolutely certain you have all had it said to you at some point in your life by a parent, family member, guardian, or teacher. Now, not to get persnickety (another brilliant word!), but usually when that phrase gets whopped out (yes, "whop" is a genuine word too), what they mean is that the person in question is obviously not content enough in their own life, otherwise they wouldn't feel the need to bring anyone else down . . . which we now know means that they are *envious* of you and the life you lead. A life that they perceive to be better than theirs. In conclusion:

Jealous = Feeling replaced
Envious = Wanting something you don't have

Although, I don't advise pointing this out to anyone in your best Hermione-Granger-know-it-all voice, as it makes people want to avoid you like the plague. I learned that the hard way.

Linguistics aside, the basic point your ever-so-wise elders are trying to make is probably right. Annoying, isn't it?

8

How to Handle a Bully

EVERY NOW AND THEN, at my Hogwarts school, we had something called a "Critical Thinking Day." All us girls thought they were the best days EVER because it meant we had no lessons and we'd spend the day "thinking critically," which somehow meant learning to count to ten in Japanese or how to juggle. How that was thinking critically I don't know, but I wasn't going to be the one to tell that to the teachers. We'd all be gathered into the hall, separated into teams of four or five, and then be given a set of challenges by some sort of motivational speaker for teenagers. At the end of the day, we'd be told the ranking orders of all the teams based on how many points we'd scored throughout the challenges. On this particular day, we were allowed to pick our own teams so "Nemesis" and her gang grouped up and all of a sudden there was this little feeling in my belly that this could turn out to be a rotten day. After a whole day of not really thinking very critically, her team won, and they trotted up to collect their winnings (a bag of fun-size chocolate bars) with a flick of the hair and an almost slow-motion, wind-machine walk.

"It's like that scene in *Mean Girls* when the Plastics walk in slow-mo down the school corridor," I whispered to my best friend.

"I bet they cheated," another girl in my team whispered back.

And that was the end of the conversation. Yet somehow, when it eventually, inevitably, got back to *her*, as all things do in schools filled with gossipers, it was being said that I had accused them of cheating and thought they all looked plastic. Not quite right, but suddenly there she was, standing over my table, asking, "Why did you say we cheated? That girl over there just said *you* said we cheated. Do you think my face looks plastic then? How dare you say we cheated? My plastic friends don't think we cheated and they all told me *you* think we did." She was loud, aggressive and showed no signs of letting up. I ended up shouting at her, through tears, to LEAVE ME ALONE. The whole room went silent . . . and then she burst out *laughing*. I'd never been so mortified. I climbed over two desks to get out of the room more quickly, ran all the way down to the toilets, and locked myself in a cubicle. I thought the worst of it was over when suddenly, BANG, BANG, BANG! Four heads popped over the cubicle walls.

"The Plastics are here!" they all bellowed, standing on the toilet seats to get a good look at me and my tear-stained face. I bolted and ran almost head first into a sixth former I was good friends with. She marched me straight to the head of the lower school, who in turn marched me straight to the school counselor.

If I'm ever asked if I was bullied when I was younger, this is the scenario that instantly springs to mind, because it was the worst I'd ever felt while I was at school. Back then, I wasn't aware of how easy I would find it, in the future, to pass off bullies as silly little children with as many insecurities as there are people who fill the seats in London's West End each night. Back then, I assumed that you just put up with bullying as best you could, stuck it out to the end of school, through the tears and the harmful thoughts, and hope it would be over when school ended. Now, however (I HATE HINDSIGHT!), I'm able to compile a little list of tips, for anybody who wants it, on how to handle those pesky bullies.

1. PUNCH THEM IN THE FACE!

Kidding! Kidding! Rule number one: Violence is never the answer. If you're going to fight, fight with your mind, not with your fists.

2. AGREE WITH THEM

Whatever they say, just politely agree.

"You're an ugly idiot!" Yes I am!

"You've got no friends!" I know, it's a shame, isn't it.

"You pick your nose and eat it!" It's a delicious, nutritious meal!

By agreeing, you're minimizing what the bully can pick on. They're looking for hidden insecurities that you don't want anyone to see, so if you openly admit and agree to them all, it becomes boring. It's also a double bluff if the bully happens to land on something that's true. They'll think it isn't true if you tell them honestly that it is, because who would do that?

3. DO NOT RETALIATE

It doesn't matter what they say to you. As soon as you start throwing abuse back, they have something to hold against you, and you run the risk of sinking to their level and becoming a bully yourself. Maintain the moral high ground. You're untouchable up there!

4. STAY CALM

Nothing spells disaster like wetting yourself in the face of a bully. Just keep in mind what I said earlier—this bully leads a much sadder life than you. They're drawing attention to your insecurities to draw attention away from their own. They're far more damaged than you are, so don't let yourself be damaged further by breaking down. You are far stronger than them. That's obvious just from the fact that they are a bully. If you feel panicky, concentrate on your breathing until your heart rate starts to slow down.

5. TELL SOMEONE

This is the *most important thing*. Even if you think you can handle the bully and the situation yourself, pull a teacher aside after school or speak to your parents. Even if no immediate action is taken, at least they're aware of it and they'll be able to keep an eye on whoever is causing the problem. If you feel uncomfortable telling an adult about it, then tell a friend, and maybe after speaking to them you can then talk to someone in authority together. If you really don't feel comfortable talking to a parent or a teacher, there are lots of responsible adults who are part of organizations or charities who are happy to speak to you anonymously and confidentially. If you want to contact them, there's a section in the back of this book FULL of links and contact details. I hope you find you're able to speak to them.

Unfortunately, bullying doesn't stop after you leave school. I thought it did, but I found out the hard way that it doesn't. Bullies exist at work, within families, on the Internet, and sometimes you even find yourself being pushed around by complete strangers. It's all part of that stupid sentence: "Life isn't fair," but if it's any comfort, I've found that the older you get, the easier it becomes to (a) ignore it, because petty insults don't affect you as much or (b) tell someone, because you want it over as soon as possible to resume everyday life. And if you are older and finding it hard to deal with a bully, the tips above still apply.

Being bullied is always going to suck, but as long as we know how to deal with it responsibly and respectfully, we can always find a way to survive it.

9

How To Identify If You're a Bully

THIS IS TOUGH. No one wants to admit they're a bully or that they've dabbled in bullying in the past—or even in the present. But it's surprising how many people don't realize that they're victimizing and intimidating people for their own gain or amusement; it just doesn't click in their brains that *that* is bullying. The rise of the Internet and social media has also made it easier to bully and harder to identify bullying. People who have never met in real life join forces over similar interests and opinions to gang up against people who, again, they have never met, and who have opposing opinions. I want to talk (rant . . .) about the Internet more later, but the point, for now, is that it makes bullying far easier. As I said earlier, bullies like to draw attention away from what's wrong with them by pointing out what they perceive to be wrong with you. Online, no one has to know who you are, so it's much easier for an anonymous account with a profile picture of a cat with its head stuck in a melon to pick on someone else who is *also* anonymously online.

Sometimes people do things in what they think is a good-natured way, not realizing how it makes other people feel. They aren't meaning to be vicious or hurt people's feelings, but they word things in a particular way, or act in a certain way, which makes people feel victimized. So, I'm hoping that this chapter may make a few more people aware of how they treat their friends (or anyone really!) and whether how they've acted in the past could have led to someone feeling hurt.

COMEDY

The bullies I've known in my time have often thought of themselves as comedians. But not in the fun, Jimmy Fallon kind of way where they prance around the classroom, making their school friends laugh about incomprehensible song lyrics and the silly things their parents say. The laughs they receive are usually based on cruel, observational humor targeted at timid or socially awkward classmates. It's lazy humor because it relies on nothing more than pointing out something that is in plain sight and, often, something the person on the receiving end of the "joke" doesn't want pointed out.

There was a girl I went to school with for five years who had a body odor issue, as a lot of young, growing teens do. Her parents had clearly not taught her about deodorant, and she hadn't picked up on her own strong odor. At first, no one mentioned it. We were all a little embarrassed for her, and we didn't know how to approach the subject delicately with her, so we simply left it. But the longer it went on, the funnier it became to us. If one of us had to sit next to her in class, our friends would snigger at us behind open textbooks. If we were paired with her in PE, our classmates would giggle as they ran past the two of us getting sweatier and smellier. The longer it went on, the less tactful we became.

One day, a drain had backed up at school and was causing one building to smell pretty foul. I walked into my classroom at lunchtime to find a few girls sitting around chatting. Now, these girls tolerated me but, all in all, they probably thought I was a little weird. I read at lunchtimes instead of socializing with them or texting the lads from the local boys' school. When shoe-shopping trips were organized, I turned them down because that wasn't really my thing. So, on this day, I saw my chance to make them laugh and warm to me a little bit. I walked into the room and made a ridiculous comment about how the bad smell wasn't really coming from the drains at all. It was coming from that poor girl. To my dismay no one laughed. *That's odd*, I thought. *They're the type of girls who always laugh about that kind of thing!* What I'd failed to notice was the girl in question was actually sitting right there, in that very room, but hidden behind someone else—I just couldn't see her from where I was standing. I only realized she was there when she got up and left the room, looking rather upset—and quite rightly so. The blood drained from my face and I immediately ran after her to apologize, and I spent the rest of my lunch hour with her trying to make her feel better. It was at that moment that I realized *I'd* just bullied someone. I'd made someone feel like crap in front of a lot of other people for my own gain, and that was a really lousy thing to do. It shouldn't matter if you think the comedy value is greater than how bad it will make someone feel. Do you really want to be the cause of someone's tears? The cause of someone's heartbreak? Or, in extreme cases, like I often read in the newspapers, the cause of someone seriously hurting themselves?

I used lazy humor to try to be popular and it backfired, big time. It wasn't worth the way I'd made someone feel, not to mention the way it made *me* feel, and I'm so glad I was able to make up for it and even consider that girl a friend (and vice versa!) for the rest of my school life. Many bullies, the ones who are aware of their bullying antics, won't feel such remorse. So, if you find yourself using humor at someone else's expense and don't want to be considered a bully, it may be a good idea to stop.

LAUGHING

Are you that person laughing at the lazy humor? If so, that makes you as much a part of the bullying as the person telling the joke. Say you were at school and you walked past a classroom in which you saw a boy punching another classmate for refusing to do his homework for him. If you walked on by with the knowledge that someone was being physically hurt without alerting anyone to it, you're as much a part of the problem as the person throwing the punches. You're endowed with the power to stop someone's pain, and you've washed your hands of it because "it's not your problem." It's the same with laughing. When someone makes a joke at someone else's expense, what really packs the punch is the laughter that follows. It's knowing that other people find your misfortune funny and are willing to laugh in your face about it that really hurts. Stop laughing, start helping. Alert someone to the situation, or get the recipient of the joke out of the firing line, talk to them, and let them know they have a friend and not everyone is out to make them feel bad.

Also, if your friend is the comedian and you don't agree with the way they're trying to get cheap laughs at the expense of someone else's feelings, it may be wise to have a quiet word with them when you're alone together. Tell them that if being funny really matters to them, they might want to try to find another way that is more considerate toward other people. I once had that conversation with a friend of mine who was making jokes at the expense of another friend of ours. I emailed him and explained that isolating and potentially losing a close friend wasn't worth the "respect" he gained from complete strangers on the Internet. Unfortunately, my friend decided it *was* worth it and, needless to say, we don't really speak all that much now.

The same rule applies when it comes to repeating mean gossip about someone. Just because it wasn't you who *started* the rumor, it doesn't mean you're blameless if you are involved in spreading it.

MANIPULATION

How often do you get your own way? And if you do, is it because you've made your case and put across your opinion so well that the other person has come round to seeing it the same way that you do? Or is it because you said or did something you knew the other person couldn't refuse?

I have a good friend called Lizzie, but while we were at school we had a falling out. One day after a school concert in which I had just played Elphaba and was painted a sickly shade of green, I asked Lizzie if she could get my bag from the balcony seats where I'd left it earlier.

"No," she said.

"What? Why?"

"I'm fed up of you constantly bossing me around and making me feel bad when I don't do things your way!"

Suddenly, everything I'd ever asked of Lizzie hit me like a ton of memory bricks (which aren't as heavy as normal bricks, but I reckon they hurt a lot more!). I would ask her to take my homework book to a teacher's pigeon hole seeing as "she was going there anyway." I'd ask to borrow her textbooks during lessons because "Why would she want to get me in trouble?" I'd constantly ask her for things and give an excuse or a reason that would make it seem like she would be a bad person if she turned me down. But what was worse was that I'd convinced myself that those excuses and reasons were true as well. It was only when she stood up for herself that I realized how horrid I'd been. From then on, when I had something that needed doing, even if Lizzie was doing it anyway, we'd do it together rather than her shouldering my weight as well. I think, again, it was to do with laziness. I found opportunities for Lizzie to do menial chores for me when, in truth, they were the tasks that took the least effort anyway, and I was more than capable of taking two minutes out of my day to do them myself.

Everyone's personality is different, and while some will simply respond to your requests with "Do it yourself, cheeky!" others are more sensitive, or more vulnerable. That's not a bad thing! It's just part of who they are, and it can be an amazing trait. But it means they may succumb more easily to being manipulated by strong personalities and will be too scared to say no, even if saying no wouldn't really upset you all that much. Be sensitive toward your friends, and especially to those who are more timid and less able to tell you to sod off when they don't want to do what you can so easily do yourself. Don't get me wrong—it's entirely fine to ask a friend for a favor! But it's only fine if you return the favor when the time comes and you're not constantly asking more of them than they ask of you. On the other hand, if you have a friend who you feel is being slightly bossy or asking you to do things they could definitely do themselves and it's making you feel a bit uncomfortable, don't be scared to tell them exactly that. If they're your true friend, they'll probably feel mortified that you feel that way and make a change immediately. If they kick up a fuss, well, they may need to work on the whole friendship thing.

MOB MENTALITY

Sometimes, we act differently when in a group of people than we do on our own. When we fit into a group, it's usually because we bring something to the table that no one else has, and when we interact with that group, we usually play up that strength. We take on the role of the gang leader or the rebel or the clown or the brains.

But sometimes, we act differently to fit into a group by mimicking each other, behaving as a group rather than as individuals. For instance, have you ever noticed that there's someone your group has decided you *all* hate and you don't really know why?

There was this group of about six girls who usually hung out together at school, one of whom—the leader—was the "nemesis" I keep referring to. As a group, they tended to stay away from me or, if they did pay me attention, they'd laugh at that one specific girl's "jokes" about me. But individually, they actually got on quite well with me. They'd follow their ringleader when she was there, but when we were alone and each girl's independent thought had miraculously kicked back in, we'd be fine.

For a while, my best friend at school, Hannah, became pally with this group, and during drama class they accepted Hannah into their group to perform with. While I was over at Hannah's house one weekend, she got a call inviting her over to the ringleader's house with the rest of the group to practice for the performance of their scene the coming week. Hannah said she was hanging out with me, and so I was invited along as well. When we got there, we found one of the girls had brought one of the biggest bars of chocolate I'd ever seen for everyone to share. So, the leader of the group inevitably took charge, grabbed the chocolate, and started to break off pieces and hand them out. When she came to me, she walked straight past and then carried on handing it out to her friends. I wasn't even bothered about the chocolate; it was just her obvious act of hatred for me in front of lots of other people that made me feel rubbish. BUT, here's the interesting thing. When her mum called her downstairs, the girl who'd brought the chocolate over—who I really got on with when we had Religious Studies together—grabbed the bar, snapped me off a chunk and shoved it in my hand. I thanked her, but all she said was, "Eat it before she gets back!" I appreciated the gesture, but it was very confusing to be on the receiving end of such mixed messages, and I just couldn't figure out why they all felt the need to act like part of a hive mind when the queen bee was around!

If you realize that your social group has shunned someone in your class, question why that is and if one person's issues are affecting the whole dynamic.

> **If you realize that your social group has shunned someone in your class, question why.**

As I've touched on already, this can be a particular problem online, where people tend to form gangs against those who don't think the same way. Remember, you're an individual with your own moral code and your own thoughts and ideas about how people should be treated. So, just because someone else thinks they can get away with being mean online in the name of your fandom of choice, don't jump on the bandwagon. The more weight that wagon gains, the more likely it is to swerve off course!

ANONYMITY

While mob mentality sometimes brings out the worst in us, individual anonymity can have a similarly negative effect. When we're able to say what we think without it being traced back to us, we get this little glimmer of mischief bubbling inside. Again, this is often an Internet-based thing, so I will cover it in more detail when we get to that section, but for now, let me just say that if you are ever given the chance to be anonymous, think about the kind of person you are and the kind of person you want to be, and keep within those moral guidelines that you've already drawn for yourself. Just because you're suddenly anonymous doesn't mean you have become a different person and can abandon your own moral code. Stay true to you, whether your face is hidden or not.

We all make mistakes and do stupid things every once in a while, and I'm not trying to say that you're a full-on bully if you have, from time to time, found yourself giggling at a mean joke or repeating a rumor, but it's worth remembering that sometimes we do partake in bullying without realizing that that's what we're doing. Growing up is about figuring out what's right and what's wrong, and often the way to do that is by unknowingly making the mistake, realizing it, rectifying it, and learning not to do it again. The sooner we realize it, the quicker we can stop that kind of behavior before we turn into fully fledged, fluffy-haired trolls.

10

The Rumor Mill

A FEW TIMES IN MY LIFE, people have asked me to keep big secrets. They've given me information that no one else has and have trusted me not to pass it on. But what if I think someone else needs that information, for whatever reason? Or the secret includes someone else and I think they deserve to know? Nay, they have a *right* to know? Well, they may well have a right to know but I have no right to pass it on. No one but the person a secret is about has a right to divulge that secret.

But it's not really *a secret. They didn't specifically say not to tell anyone! It's hardly a BIG secret!*

Shush, Carrie. None of that matters. It is not your secret, therefore you have to keep mum. Except . . .

When I was younger, I had a friend who told me a big secret. And I mean *big*. Bigger than any two teenagers should ever have had to manage. The weight of it dragged us down for weeks and, ultimately, impacted our friendship. I swore I wouldn't tell this secret to a soul, and I didn't. I promised I would take the secret to my grave (and I'm willing to stand by that, so I'm certainly not going divulge it in this book). But I knew if she didn't tell *someone* it would get worse and worse, and she'd be scared all her life that someone would find out. I encouraged her to tell her mum, and at the time I felt that was all I could do. Eventually, someone else found out. My friend thought I'd let it slip, and she never fully trusted me again. To this day I think she's still carrying that secret around like the world on her shoulders.

Although, ninety-nine percent of the time, I would say that you should *never* reveal someone else's secret, even if you don't agree with what they're doing or wish that they would tell more people, I do regret this specific incident. At the time, I felt that I did everything I could do without betraying my friend's trust, but sometimes secrets are *big. Too* big. So humongous that someone of authority *needs* to be told, whether it's your secret or not. My friend could have been in real peril, and also needed huge amounts of emotional support. My regret is that I wish I had told an adult. Someone in authority who could have helped and lifted the weight from both our shoulders. That secret was far too big and dangerous for two girls of our age and we *needed* someone's help and, because we never asked for it, we'll carry that secret to our graves and it'll weigh us down forever. If you find yourself in a similar situation, ask yourself: If I keep this secret, am I putting myself or my friend in harm's way? Don't break someone's trust lightly—don't tell their secret just because it will make your life easier. But if they are in danger or if it's a burden that you think will haunt them forever, then do share it with an adult *you* trust.

When secrets are my own, I can't contain them. I am the worst for telling people in July what I've bought them for Christmas. I'm also really prone to telling people things about myself that I don't feel are secrets, but they're things other people would want to keep secret if the information was theirs, so that I end up the center of idle gossip. For instance, when I was seventeen I told my friends that I wasn't a virgin. I'd been in a relationship with my boyfriend for over a year and, to be honest, I didn't think the news would come as a huge shock to anyone. It soon spread around school but, like a good game of telephone, the rumor ended up being that I'd slept with eleven boys over the summer and probably, even definitely, had chlamydia. Oh, gossip, how I hate you so! But that's the thing about it. The more a rumor is spread, the further it gets from the truth. It's like a giant taffy pull. The truth gets put on the hook and then stretched and strained of any truth; it gets bigger and more elaborate with every pull and becomes an entirely different story (and if you don't get that analogy then you've never tried taffy and, man . . . you NEED to try taffy!). Each time, the protagonist is a little more "larger than life," doing extraordinary things, and when people eventually find out that's not what actually happened at all, they decide the true story is boring and carry on spreading the juicier version.

It's hard to handle being gossiped about. The rumor is either something that's true that you don't want to admit to, or it's something that's got an inch of truth but has been stretched so far the story has a million holes in it (that everyone's ignoring, so your explanation will most likely be ignored too). OR the rumor is not even the slightest bit true and every time you shout at the top of your lungs, "IT'S NOT TRUE!" that annoying little twerp in the corner peeps out from behind their copy of *Othello*, pushes their glasses up their nose, and says, "I think thee doth protest too much!"

In the case of a rumor about you that is one hundred percent, absolutely, posi-tute-ly not true being spread like wildfire, why give it any fuel? Ignore the hell out of it. Technically it's not actually even about you if it's not true, so let them talk to their hearts' content. What's it going to change?

The best way to combat the arse-face that is gossip is to (a) keep your mouth tightly shut when you're entrusted with a secret, (b) firmly seal your lips when someone passes on a rumor, (c) if you think the secret is causing harm to you or other people, encourage its owner to talk to someone who can help, and (d) if it's your own secret, think hard about how it could be spread and misconstrued and rethink whether it's a good idea to share it and/or who you're sharing it with.

If you feel a secret, whether it's yours or a friend's, is too big and potentially harmful, don't tell your friends and run the risk of gossip spreading; keep mum to your peers but speak to a responsible and authoritative adult (be it a teacher, parent, or police officer) or contact one or more of the links listed in the back of the book.

11

The Art of Biting Your Tongue

I TALK A LOT BOTH ONLINE AND IN REAL LIFE about how it upsets me when people can't be civil to one another. I'm very aware that everyone is different and we all have a million and one reasons for not liking whoever it is we don't like, but there's a big difference between how we THINK and how we ACT. We think bad thoughts every day, whether we purposefully mean to or not, but unless we voice them, no one has to know they were there. Sure, your conscience may take a beating for the fact you even thought something bad in the first place, but that's as far as the damage has to go.

I used to be *great* at saying whatever was in my head. The good, the bad, and the downright mad. My friends and I used to joke that my head was like a coffee machine that had lost its filter. Whatever went in slipped straight out, unfiltered, full of gunky, weird coffee-bean grime. However, in time, after some awful run-ins with friends, teachers, and even my parents, I realized that I was actually in control of my own mouth. What a shock. I used to be so confused about why people got annoyed at the things I said and blamed THEM for being too oversensitive rather than myself for being a bit of a clod. Eventually, through sheer experience and just maturing a little bit, I realized the difference between *thinking* something and actually *saying* it and how I could avoid pissing people off. It suddenly seemed so simple.

And it does seem so easy written down in one teeny weeny paragraph. *Too* easy, even. It also *sounds* easy when you say it out loud! It's not. I can assure you, it's not. It's as hard as riding a unicycle while juggling three chimps and a watermelon. But it *is* possible with enough willpower, and walking away from a conversation with someone you don't like feels so much better knowing you've been perfectly respectful and you didn't rise to whatever bait they laid out for you. It doesn't matter if they're someone who often tries to provoke you into fighting with them or if they're someone who just occasionally rubs you the wrong way for whatever reason. There is absolutely no excuse for not being civil.

It isn't easy at first. When faced with someone who is just dying for a fight, it's hard not to bite back. Just like riding a unicycle while juggling three chimps and a watermelon, it's hard not to fall off when trying to get it right. Regret wouldn't exist if most people in this world hadn't said or done things in spontaneous, heated arguments that they wish they could take back or rewind. I, personally, don't like confrontation or causing a rumpus, and I especially don't like hurting people's feelings, so I've definitely learned a few valuable lessons over the years about biting my tongue. The main thing I always try to remember when I'm seeing red is that, after the moment passes, whatever is it that has made me angry won't matter even half as much as it once did, and when it's all just a memory I'll be happy that I didn't say anything to make an already crappy situation worse.

You don't have to like everyone. No one is holding you to being the world's best human being. Likewise, not everyone is going to like you (and that's probably harder to deal with). But you will feel like a happier, better person if you try to be civil to everyone. It doesn't matter how awful you think they are or whatever they've done in the past to aggravate you. Don't give them a reason not to like you or to hold anything against you later on. I think "irreproachable" is the word. If you remain civil and respectful, you are faultless.

However, I can tell you from my own experiences that people tend to confuse learning to bite my tongue with being fake. They seem to think I'm not being genuine when in fact I'm being polite to someone that I don't really get on with to avoid unnecessary conflict. But say, for instance . . .

There's someone at a party you tend not to get on well with, and most of the other people at the party know you aren't particularly keen on each other. You're both reaching for the same . . . let's say sausage roll (because the only kinds of parties I know are the ones with sausage rolls, jelly, and ice cream. I don't get asked out much . . .) and you have no choice but to acknowledge their presence in some way. Do you:

(a) Blatantly ignore them, making the atmosphere unnecessarily prickly for you both and those who happen to witness the moment

(b) Acknowledge their presence by making some snide remark based on the last argument you had, which then drags up the past

Or (c) Say hello, perhaps even smile nicely, because what harm can it do and what extra effort does it take to be courteous to someone standing beside you, no matter who they are or what has happened in the past? The ball is then in their court to acknowledge your pleasantries in any manner they choose and you can walk away from the experience knowing you tried to be pleasant and peaceful.

(There is also secret option (d) Try to drown them in the punch bowl. But that one might be too hard to resist, so I thought it best not to add it in . . .)

The key to being civil is also being sincere. Don't wish them a good day if what you secretly mean is "I want to punch you in the face." You'll say it through gritted teeth or with an accidental sarcastic tone, and it won't do anyone any good. It's hard to get over the initial idea of being civil to someone who you don't think deserves it, but they are another human being, after all. That civil sincerity needs to come from realizing that even though you, personally, may not like them, it doesn't necessarily make them a bad person, and they still deserve to be treated like a human being.

It doesn't take much to be outwardly pleasant to anyone, even if the history you've had with that one particular person has been less than desirable, and the way you feel toward them could definitely be perked up a tad. Especially when you're in the company of mutual friends who would rather not have to deal with issues that aren't theirs, it's not being fake, it's being civil—and taking the thoughts and feelings of the other people around you into consideration. Basically, it's what people mean when they say "be the bigger person."

ACT 3

How to Get Your Heart Broken Only Just a Little Bit

12

The Disgusting Business of Falling in Love

LOVE HAS ALWAYS FASCINATED ME. It's such a forceful, all-consuming power, and I've definitely succumbed to it a handful of times in my life. And, gosh, I've never known something to be so gleefully wonderful and soul-crushingly exhausting before. It's brilliant and awful. Healing and painful. It can make you grow into a better person or crush you into a bitter one all at the same time, and it's completely unexplainable.

There's nothing quite like feeling yourself falling in love. You ask yourself all these questions: Is it a good thing? Is it bad? Do they feel the same? Will it amount to anything in the end? In three years' time, when I'm with someone else, will I look back and think, *What an idiot!?* Am I wasting my time? Meanwhile, no matter what any of the answers are, you're falling. Slowly but surely sinking down that rabbit hole, knowing you're either going to hit the bottom painfully, letting your heart clatter and shatter into a million tiny jagged pieces which you'll have to collect and glue back together while simultaneously clawing your way back *out* of that rabbit hole. *Or* that special person will be there to catch you at the bottom, ready to whisk you off on an adventure in your own personal wonderland.

Whenever I've been on the verge of falling—looking into that rabbit hole from the surface and feeling my hands starting to slip against the grassy, muddy edges, with the earth beginning to crumble under my fingertips—I always ask myself, *Is this right? Is this really what I should be doing?* But it doesn't matter because what can I do to stop it? That earth is going to crack and give way whether I like it or not, and I won't know what the outcome will be until I've reached the bottom. It's the strangest feeling knowing that falling in love may not be the best thing to do and could result in your heart

being broken. You just have to hope that the other person is falling in love with you too, so that when you finally reach solid ground, you're both there for each other to soften the blow.

Falling in love is a scary and sometimes brutal business. I sometimes wish I didn't have to bother with it, but being a human being I guess I don't have much choice in the matter. The amount of times I've said to myself, after having had my heart broken for the gazillionth time, *RIGHT! That's it.* No more. *I need to think about myself for a while and not indulge in any romance in any way, shape, or form!* And then suddenly a boy comes into my life from out of absolutely sodding nowhere and there I go again. Going all weak at the knees and goggly eyed. I genuinely start to annoy myself with my own sickeningly sweet, lovey-dovey thoughts . . . but then again I enjoy that giddy, schoolgirlish feeling so much that it's this war in my head between the part of me that thinks, *Oh come on, it's lovely feeling like this. Enjoy it while it lasts!* and the part of me that's shouting, *But when it comes to an end you're gonna hate yourself for having indulged in feeling this way, so you may as well just pack it in now!* It's a very confusing thing and because I've found I can't just switch off feeling that way, the lovey-dovey part of me wins every time.

No matter how many times I've had my heart broken, though, I will always be glad for the time I spent being in love because, let's be honest, there's nothing else quite like it. When you can feel your smile stretch just that little bit further over the simplest of things: a kiss on the forehead, a word said just the right way, or a glance that lasted a few seconds longer than it should have. When you tingle all over when they kiss you or touch you, like you've been kissed by an electric eel! And if heartbreak follows, well, it's just proof that you were doing it right. You were loving with everything you had, and that's why it hurts so much when the person you were loving isn't there to love any more. I truly believe that the amount you hurt is equal to the amount you loved that person, so if it's really hurting, at least take comfort in the knowledge that you are capable of loving and caring about someone that much. That's a truly amazing thing. You should be proud of it. You'll be able to find the strength to love someone just that much again once you've recovered from this heartbreak. It just takes time.

> If heartbreak follows, well, it's just proof that you were doing it right.

Falling in love can be really tricky and messy and downright disgusting at times, but while you're in it and—if it doesn't work out—once your heart has mended a bit and you look back at it, there's no denying that overall it's a pretty beautiful thing.

13

The Birds and the Bees

DON'T YOU THINK "THE BIRDS AND THE BEES" sounds like the name of a pub? Although perhaps one that no one would ever drink in. (It'd be the perfect place for bachelor/ette parties . . .) Anyway, I have no idea why we call "it" that. Birds don't get it on with bees . . . do they?

So, I'm going to assume that you are all aware that TBATB is code for the talk your parents have with you when you're a kid—the one about *sex*. I hope I'm not being too presumptuous, but I'm also going to assume that your parents have already had that talk with you and you're well aware that sex is when two people love each other very much and have a "special hug." We're all clear on that, right? What I want to talk about, and what I think often gets left out of that conversation, is the *context*. The actual, specific relationship you have with your partner at the time you decide it's right to take it to the next level. Of course, your parents hate the idea of their baby growing up and doing the jiggly with some stranger they haven't met yet, when they can't even begin to guess what sort of person you'll end up with, nor the relationship you'll have together.

Relationships are never black and white. *Feelings* are never black and white. There's always a grey area, and it's in that grey area that Bella's conflicting love for two very different men (men?) lives. It's where Mr. Darcy's love for the strongheaded and penniless Elizabeth Bennett lives. It's where the disturbing and twisted Draco/Harry fan fiction that I've read (and enjoyed!) lives. There are so many ins and outs a relationship can have that it's hard to give blanket rules to cover all eventualities. No one can possibly know every kind of love there ever was and ever will be. What I'm trying to say is that when it comes to love, and sex, things can get very complicated and confusing. Lines become blurred, and sometimes boundaries are crossed.

Let me tell you a little story . . .

When I was younger I went out with a boy for a while. I don't really count him as a "proper" boyfriend, but what happened between us has always stayed with me.

We got each other's MSN messenger addresses (ahh, those were the days!) and we started talking. He was not very good-looking, not very charming, and *very* interested in sex. But to a girl who was desperate to have a boyfriend like the rest of her friends and who wanted to feel loved like in all the movies she'd watched and all the books she'd read, he was ideal, and I agreed to go on a date to the cinema with him. My two friends who came with me to meet him then went off shopping and, boy, do I wish I'd gone with them.

I'd already kissed someone before, and I was happy to have another go. Just so I could say that I had. But during the movie, he started asking me to do things that I'd never done before and was most certainly not comfortable doing at that point—certainly not in a cinema or to him. I sort of pretended I hadn't heard him and continued to watch the film while he continued to ask.

For some reason, I agreed to meet up with him again—this time at his house, where I met his mum. We went up to his room, where there was a yellow T-shirt hanging on one of his wardrobe doors.

"I bought it at a concert and don't want it. Do you?" He took it down and held it up against my front, but then shook his head. "You wouldn't look good in yellow." Looking back now, I can't believe I didn't say anything to that. Then, again, he started asking things of me that I didn't want to do. This time, I made a point of saying no. He asked, "Why?" and I shrugged and said, "*Because.*" He didn't speak to me for the rest of the day until I left to go home.

He called me up that evening and asked to see me again. I felt like I had disappointed him at his house and that I needed to redeem myself, so I agreed. We sat on the sofa watching TV and I chatted to his dad (who seemed lovely) until he went out to the shops. As soon as the front door closed, this boy tried to kiss me, but I kept refusing, until he was lying on top of me and then started asking me to "have it off" with him. How he hadn't realized that even his way of asking was enough to make any girl say no is beyond me. I continued to persistently say no and he continued to ask why. He started getting angry, and I got scared so I ran out of the room and up the stairs, but he caught me by my ankle and pulled me back down to face him. Sitting there awkwardly on the stairs, with my ankle in his grasp, I didn't feel scared but angry. I was angry that someone was treating me like this and that they thought they could get away with it. I was angry that I hadn't felt this courage back in the cinema—when I'd been so eager to prove myself to a boy who I'd think *nothing* of in years to come—to tell him to go to hell. I pushed him away with everything I had, raced up the stairs, found the bathroom, and locked myself in it.

He sat outside the bathroom door, talking through it, begging me to come out, telling me that he was sorry and didn't know what had come over him. Eventually, I came out and we went back downstairs to the sofa. A few minutes later, he was getting very close to my face and asking, "Why won't you have it off with me?" in a sad and disappointed voice. I fixed my eyes on the TV next to us and didn't say a word or look his way until we heard the front door open. He jumped away from me and plonked himself at the far end of the sofa, as if that wasn't proof enough that he already *knew* what he had been doing was wrong. That evening he called to say he thought we should break up. When I asked why, his reply was, "You're just not pretty enough for me." He had pressured me, made me feel uncomfortable and like that was my fault, showed signs of a controlling nature, and then dumped me because I didn't conform to what he perceived as pretty.*

---

* This will be the first my parents know of this story. I should have told them both at the time so they could have helped, even though the situation wasn't as severe as it potentially could have been. But I was too scared of the repercussions, because even though I hadn't, I felt like I'd done something wrong and, stupidly, I didn't want the guy to get in trouble! So, Mum and Dad, when you get to this bit in the book, Mum, if you're crying, you're a wally. And, Dad, no I don't know where he lives now, so you can't kill him. Sorry! Stop worrying, I'm TOTALLY fine, I love you both, and enjoy the rest of the book your daughter's written. ;-)

For a thirteen-year-old, this experience was pretty scary and, sadly, I know it's a scenario that's repeated, in different situations and to different degrees, far more frequently than many people realize. I was able to walk away from this situation relatively unscathed, but plenty of people don't.

In an ideal relationship, there are two equal people who both make each other feel loved, understood, considered, and, most of all, safe, and because of that wonderful safe environment they will also feel completely comfortable saying what they do and don't want to happen—not just when it comes to potential sexual acts, but within their entire relationship. I'm relieved to say that the majority of my own relationships have been like this, and it's such a lovely place to be.

After that guy, I didn't really have much interaction with boys again, what with being at an all-girls school, until I was sixteen and I joined a production of *Les Misérables* (I can't get enough of that show!) at Harrow School, which is famously known as the school Winston Churchill went to. (It's also where some of Harry Potter was filmed!) It's there where I met my first "proper" boyfriend who was hugely respectful of not just me but everyone. We were each other's "firsts," but not once did he pressure me or make me feel uncomfortable, and he regularly told me that I had to tell him if anything within our relationship was moving too fast. He was an absolute gem and we stayed together for two and a half years. Our relationship fizzled out eventually, and we parted as friends. We still meet for lunch every few months at what used to be our favorite restaurant.

But not all relationships are as loving or as understanding as we'd like them to be—for a whole plethora of reasons. To make this a little easier, I'm going to split the rest of this chapter up into sections consisting of little things to remember whenever you find yourself in a sexual situation with someone, or if you're ever unsure about the way you're being treated by your partner or advised by those around you, who are looking in at your relationship from the outside.

YOUR BODY IS YOURS

We all come to the point when our bodies are suddenly desired by other people, and that can be a lovely feeling. But your body belongs to *you* and everything you do with it is *your* decision. It is your decision whether someone kisses, touches, hugs, or has sex with you.

PRESSURE

There may be people who will try to influence your decisions about whether they get to touch you or not. They'll try to manipulate your choices by making you feel guilty or putting so much pressure on you that you eventually give in. Even if you've said yes to some things, or had sex with them before, it doesn't mean you have to say yes again. If someone is making you feel guilty for not having sexual interactions with them, or piling on the pressure until you crack, step back and ask yourself whether they are really worth spending your time and effort on.

Sex is not consensual unless both people want it. Sex is supposed to be an act between two people who love and trust each other completely, and if that encounter is happening because one person manipulated the other person into it, it becomes something entirely different—something that can, depending on the circumstances, even be against the law.

CREATING A SAFE ENVIRONMENT

If you feel you are ready—within yourself and your own mind—and decide you want to take things to the next level with your partner, the best way to find out if they also feel the same way is by *asking*. And the *unbelievably important* thing you have to remember is that, whatever their answer, you have to accept it. If they say they aren't ready, you need to be OK with this. Any sexual interaction (from hugging and touching to full-blown intercourse) HAS to be OK with both parties before it occurs, and the best way to figure that out is by talking about it. Create a safe environment for your partner by letting them know that you're happy with how they feel no matter what—AND MEAN IT. Be understanding and considerate if they don't feel they are ready yet.

Being in an understanding, loving, and safe relationship means ensuring that the other person feels like they can tell you exactly what they do and do not want. You can play your part in this by asking them how they feel and if they're alright with what's happening, and ensuring you speak out when you do or don't want something to happen. It is perfectly fine for you to say no *at any point*, even if you've had sex with them before, and even if you're about to do the deed and then change your mind. You can say no WHENEVER you feel that you want to and it is perfectly OK.

HOW TO SAY "NO"

Saying "no" isn't easy, especially if it's to someone you have feelings for. Here are some tips from a great website called thesite.org (see the Props section for more information about the services and advice they offer) on how to say "no" in difficult situations.*

If your partner says to you: "If you loved me you'd do it."

Try saying: If you loved me, you (a) wouldn't have just said that and (b) would respect my decision.

If your partner says to you: "Everyone else is doing it."

Try saying: I'm not everyone else.

If your partner says to you: "You're frigid."

Try saying: No. I'm just comfortable with who I am and what I want.

If they're still pressuring you say "NO" more firmly and tell them they're making you feel uncomfortable. Get up and leave if possible—you can talk it through tomorrow when they've cooled down.

BODY LANGUAGE

Reading your partner's body language is also incredibly important. If they seem unsure or uncomfortable, don't carry on with what you're doing just because they haven't said "no" or "stop" yet. They may feel awkward stopping what's happening because they don't want to "ruin the moment" or they're scared they may sound silly or worried you'll be angry or annoyed. If they seem unsure in any way, talk to them.

---

* Thank you to Holly Bourne and YouthNet for allowing me to use this! bit.ly/thesite-sayingno

Ask them if they're OK with what's going on. Do not take their silence as a "yes."

IF YOU ARE A VICTIM

I want to be clear that if you feel you have taken part in a sexual act against your wishes, but didn't speak out or were pressured into going along with what your partner wanted, *you are not to blame* for what then happened. They are. Unfortunately, there are some people in this world who will take your silence as a "yes," or simply disregard your "no." I truly hope none of you ever find yourselves in this situation, and all I can really say is that if the person you're with won't stop and they become forceful, emotionally or physically, the last thing you should worry about is being rude or hurting their feelings. Try to remove yourself from the situation, go somewhere you feel safe and, if you can, talk to someone about what happened. Even if you are with someone you care about very much, it is not OK for them to make you feel unsafe or vulnerable, or to make you do things you're not comfortable with.

I want to encourage you to speak out and stand up to anyone who's trying to make you do something you don't want to do within your relationship, but it's not always easy to do and you mustn't blame yourself if you've ended up in a situation where you've done things you didn't want to.

If something has happened and you are struggling to deal with it, please speak to someone about it, or use the Props (or, technically speaking, the resources) section in the back of this book to find organizations who can support you.

AND FINALLY, DON'T GENERALIZE

Phew, after reading all that it may seem like every man is out to pressure you and every woman is going to manipulate you to get her way. But not everyone is like that. That's SO important to remember. In my personal experience, there are so many wonderful, considerate, and understanding people out there who are willing to treat the one they end up with in the way they deserve to be treated. Men aren't awful creatures by definition. Neither are women. Some are, I'll give you that, but if we go around thinking that every man will try to force us to have sex with him and every woman we meet wants to manipulate us into bed, we'll never have those wonderful relationships we so deserve to have.

After a rather messy break-up a while back, I had a moment of wondering whether all men are hardwired to be brutes. As quickly as that thought popped into my head, I met someone who changed my mind entirely. Someone who is so exceedingly honest that it took me a while to get used to him telling me what he thought and how he felt, and then *actually asking me how I felt and accepting the answer, whatever that was.* And it's very clear it's all sincere, too. I'm still in awe of him and his ways and I'm very grateful to know him.

So in short, we need to:
- Remember that our body is ours and we have control over what we do with it and whether someone else gets to touch it.
- Make sure our partners feel they can speak to us about anything and ask them how they feel and what they want.

- Speak out straight away if we feel uncomfortable with something that's happening, regardless of whether our partner asks us or not.
- Oh yes, and remember: ALWAYS USE PROTECTION. ALWAYS. I can't believe I nearly forgot that bit. Unless you want a little screaming sprog before you're ready which, if you're anything like me, you don't! Seriously, if you're about to start having sex, take a trip to your doctor or the local family planning clinic and get yourself kitted out with all the necessary stuff. Girls, make like a girl scout and "be prepared" with whatever contraception suits you—be it condoms, the pill, or the implant. There's loads of options so talk it through with a professional; they'll be used to it so there's no need to feel embarrassed. And, boys, girly contraception requires more forward planning than a box of condoms, so while the girls need to be prepared, so do you!

14

Let Yourself Feel Pretty

I DON'T KNOW ABOUT YOU, but I always like it when someone in the public eye is humble about their very obvious talent or beauty. It shows a certain amount of self-awareness and . . . manners. Even though they're famous, they're also down to earth and modest, and those are traits that we like to see in the people we look up to and admire. We're going to adore someone even more when they respond to being told how utterly brilliant they are with "Oh really? You think so? That's so very kind of you. Thank you so much!" rather than "Ch'yeah. I know!" Having said that, these people usually have a whole entourage of people advising them on how to respond to . . . everything, even compliments. We normal people, on the other side of the red carpet barrier, are not so lucky.

One of the problems with this "Aw shucks, me?" thing is that most celebrities *are* drop-dead gorgeous, or at least we're made to believe they are. In magazines, movies and on billboards they're posed this way and that way, made-up to the brim, lit to the max, and dressed to the nines to bring out the best of them and make them fit into the mold that society has decided is "conventionally good-looking." But what this has done is made us all feel like we need to look like that to be socially accepted, not just by everyone else, but by ourselves when we look in the mirror. We think we need to be size 6 or (much) less, have hair that falls in the perfect way, flawless glowing skin, sparkling white teeth, no bat wings or cellulite—the list goes on and on and on and on until we've convinced ourselves that nothing about us is acceptable or beautiful and we'll never be photographable or lovable, no matter how hard we try. If that doesn't sound awful enough, it leads to this conversation:

"You look very pretty today!"

"No I don't."

"No, really you do! At least, I think so anyway."

"WELL YOU'RE WRONG! I'M UGLY AND FAT AND I HATE MYSELF." *flails*

And it sucks because usually the people complimenting us are being genuine and wouldn't bother saying anything if they didn't really mean it—but we don't let them be nice to us. We don't let ourselves feel good or be open to that kind of positivity because we've been led to believe there's only ONE perfect way to look and if we're even only a smidge over the line, we're disgusting and not "normal" and we should be ashamed of ourselves for even existing. It's total bollocks. I'm sorry, but I can't think of any other way of describing the situation. It's a pair of a man's sweaty, unwashed private parts after he's run the London Marathon. Just imagine that! It's *that* awful!

LET YOURSELVES FEEL APPRECIATED. If someone tells you you're pretty (or kind, clever, or talented) believe them and thank them for telling you. The more you let yourself accept compliments, the easier it'll become to accept that maybe everyone is different, and maybe there *are* people out there who will like the way you look despite the flaws you think you have, and you'll start to feel better about yourself. Also, if someone is ever cruel or negative about you, it'll be easier to ignore because you'll be aware that there are actually people out there who think you're wonderful and you suit *their* tastes exactly. It's finding that balance between acknowledging that not everyone will like you or the way you look and knowing that other people *will*. It's not arrogant to know you're loved or to let people tell you they love the way you look, the way you think, or simply the way you *are*.

Let yourself feel special. Inside and out. Let yourself be loved for who and what you are no matter whether you're short, tall, round, slender, ginger, blonde, brunette, freckly, spotty, lanky, large, hetero-/homo-/bisexual—whatever. Give people the chance to tell you that they

> It's not arrogant to know you're loved or to let people tell you they love the way you are.

think you're lovely without cutting them down and TELL-ING them what they should think of you, because your mind has been warped by society telling you exactly how you should look. Let people make up their own minds about you, and if they pay you a compliment, pretend you're on the red carpet at a premiere and say, "Oh really? You think so? That's so very kind of you. Thank you SO much!"

15

Happy and Healthy

OK, OK, SO NOT ALL OF US GET SHOWERED WITH COMPLIMENTS day in and day out (which is all the more reason we should listen and appreciate when we do!) but that's all right because as long as we're happy within ourselves and we're healthy, that's all that should matter. Right? Because that's *so* easy! Of *course*, it's not that easy to be completely at ease in your own skin. Especially when you're a teenager and that skin is, more often than not, a bit oily and spotty and forever growing and changing around whatever shape you'll one day become. You feel lanky, gangly, too fat, too thin, and just completely disgusting.

Body image is something that so many people struggle with. Especially teenagers. (I know that lots of boys feel under pressure to look a certain way too, but I'm mainly going to talk here about how I felt as a teenage girl. I think a lot of the same things apply though.) When you're young and on the search for role models—people to look up to and aspire to be like—you're rarely given *real* images. You're given pictures that have been run through Photoshop: Bodies have been distorted, waists have been cinched, cheekbones have been sucked out, necks and legs lengthened, and lips plumped—you name it. These women have been made to look very little like how they appear in the mirror every morning. But it's very easy to take it as fact that that is what they look like in real life and, even if it isn't, surely the photo has been made to look that way because that's how they *should* look. So does that mean *I* should look like that too?

When I was fourteen, I was a little overweight. Not hugely, but enough for me to cringe a bit when I look back at pictures. I call it my "rugby player" phase. Stocky shoulders, a spare tire around my middle, and thunder thighs. But when I was that age, I never really looked at myself and thought I was fat or big. My mum was good at making me feel like I was normal, and the few friends I had at school never led me to believe I was anything other than accepted. I still knew I didn't look like *that* though—the way those movie stars look. The way those dancers look on that TV show. The way that model in that advert looks. I was constantly bombarded with images in magazines, on TV, on posters, and EVERY-WHERE of how women "should" look—the shape that men want when they're looking for a girlfriend/lover/wife. As a very lonely fourteen-year-old who wanted nothing more than to be loved by a guy, it made me feel so sad that I didn't already look that way, and I felt I was never *going* to look that way because that just wasn't me. (And the idea of having to go to the gym and do an awful lot of moving and less cake-eating didn't appeal to me!) Luckily, for me, this never developed into an eating disorder, but the scary thing is that it so easily could have and does in many teenagers. It's terrifying to think these perfectly normal, healthy, and *gorgeous* young girls and guys feel they have to squeeze themselves into these molds that the media tells us we NEED to fit into to be accepted.

Now, as I've said and will keep saying, I'm no counselor or trained professional. All I can tell you is how I've dealt with feeling insecure about my looks in the past. When I've felt all sweaty and my hair's a bit greasy and my belly looks pudgy and my feet look like a clown's and a fresh new spot has appeared right in the middle of my forehead and there's no chance in hell that anyone, not even myself, will find me in any way attractive in the slightest, it's a horrible feeling that makes me want to curl up into a ball under my duvet and not resurface until exactly the way I look has come into fashion! But I have to keep reminding myself of two things:

I am *happy*.
I am *healthy*.

So, what else matters?

Firstly, I remind myself of the other things about me that are attractive in their own right. Not attractive to other people necessarily, but things that I find attractive about me that aren't anything to do with my physical appearance. Like most people, I'm pretty good at putting myself down, but the truth is I enjoy the fact that I'm quite creative, I can sing and act, I read a lot of books, I'm a good storyteller, and I like to be nice for no reason because it gives me a huge sense of happiness and contentment. When I think of all those things I feel proud to be me. Taking aesthetics ENTIRELY out of the equation, I am proud to be me with everything I have. So, the way I look or feel in my own skin doesn't detract from everything else that I am. That thought gives me my own little confidence boost and, of course, I still feel kind of icky on occasion, but none of the things on the inside of me change and those are the things that matter the most. As I get older, my appearance is going to change and morph into the old-lady version of me. My long blonde hair is going to turn grey, the years of laughing and crying are going to catch up to my eyes and cause the skin to wrinkle and crack, and all the cake I've eaten (and it's A LOT of cake . . .) is going to decide, actually, it *does* want to go straight to my bum! But the fact that I like to leave notes around London with nice things written on them to make other people smile, the paintings and drawings I do in my spare time, and all the books I've read and will read . . . none of that is going to change, and that makes me extremely happy. So, ask yourself, what do you find most attractive about yourself that has nothing to do with aesthetics? What traits of your personality make you proud to be you? Because if you've got that, what does it matter that you think your skin's a bit spotty? Those spots don't make any kind of a mark on the person you are on the inside, and being lovely on the inside is far more important than being lovely on the outside. And there are people in the world who will see that in you—but it's crucial that you see that in yourself first. There are so many people who are gorgeous on the outside and just plain ugly on the inside, and it's those people that end up alone because if you treat people badly, it just doesn't matter how beautiful you are.

Secondly, are you healthy? If you're a healthy weight and size for your age, don't let anyone else tell you that you should be something other than what you already are. If you are uncomfortable with the way that you are, that's for you to decide and for you to change in a healthy way by eating better or exercising a bit more. But never let anyone tell you that you should be something other than you are if you're already healthy and happy. The media can be mean and plant an idea of perfection in your head that just isn't realistic because it's created by Photoshop. If you *do* feel uncomfortable with your body image, talk to someone about it. A parent, a friend, a doctor, or someone you trust. When we start to grapple with insecurities like this, that awful little voice in your head can start to ask questions like "What if no one else understands? What if it's just me that feels this way? Is there something wrong with me? Should I hide it and deal with it on my own?" It can become unhealthy and develop in very damaging ways, so it's best to talk about it to someone you trust who can help you deal with it in a way that maintains your health and your happiness.

I uploaded a video on my YouTube channel on this subject around December 2013, after someone sent a message to my Tumblr inbox to say they were really worried about their weight. She felt like she was overweight, and was being made fun of by her peers. When I replied and told her that I was the same age, weight, and height, she messaged back in disbelief. "NO WAY!" she wrote. "I've always watched your videos and thought you looked not too big, not too small. A healthy size but I always thought I was sooooo much bigger! To know we're almost exactly the same size has given me a boost in confidence!" Immediately, I whacked out my pen and notebook and started writing out notes for a video in which I would take my own measurements on camera and reveal them to my audience. I didn't want to make it sound like I was the perfect weight and size to aspire to, because I'm not. I've always thought I could definitely lose a couple of pounds or so because I do eat an extortionate amount of cakes and sweets that will catch up with me one day, but I am a healthy weight for my age and height, and if that one girl felt a boost in confidence because she turned out to be the same size as someone she thought was much slimmer than her, maybe others would feel that same boost too! It was worth a shot and it's still worth a shot now!

Age: 22
Height: 5 foot 5 inches
Waist: 26 inches
Hips: 40 inches
Bust: 34 inches
Bra Size: 34B
Weight: 149 pounds

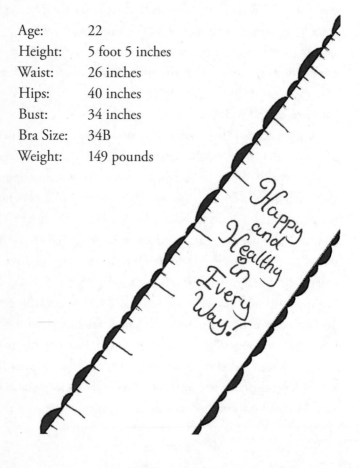

Happy and Healthy in Every Way!

16

How NOT to Handle a Break-Up

BRACE YOURSELVES, GUYS. I'm going to impart some hard-won knowledge: *There is no "right way" to handle a break-up.* (In fact, there is no "right way" to handle any difficult situation—take a look at Chapter 27 to see what I mean.) We're all unique, individual people, and every relationship is entirely different from the last, so the way *you* might handle a break-up is going to be miles and miles away from how *I*, or anyone else, might react in a similar situation.

In my life, I've had a couple of big relationships that I would call "proper" relationships when I'm in casual conversation with friends. Those relationships went slightly awry somewhere along the way and ended with the inevitable break-up. So let me tell you this: Break-ups Suck. They majorly, massively suck like a giant hoover! The first of my break-ups was my own doing. I'd fallen out of love and couldn't continue on in a relationship that I wasn't happy in because it wasn't fair to either of us. This was easier to deal with because it was my decision, and the boy in question was extremely understanding and wanted what was best and fair for the both of us too.

I spent that night crying over my lost future (more on that in Chapter 17), wailing inconsolably into my pillows, and then had to do the miserable deed of changing my relationship status on various different social media profiles from "IN A BLISSFULLY HAPPY RELATIONSHIP!" to "Sad, alone, and single ☹." There are few things as humiliating and heart-breaking as when you watch that little heart on Facebook become two jagged halves of a whole. I wrote a brief status letting my family and friends know that, after two and a half years, the boy in question and I were amicably breaking up. I resorted to telling them via social media because I was too sad and embarrassed to admit that a relationship I was once so happy and proud of had come to an end. It was my way of saying "Don't mention this again until a considerable amount of time has passed, because I will just cry into your shoulder for an hour if you do." I then texted my mum, who was sitting on the sofa downstairs watching *Emmerdale*, and told her it'd be nice to be alone for an evening. I was very afraid that if she opened my bedroom door she'd be flooded by a salty tidal wave of my tears and snot, so I warded her off as best I could.

The second break-up was the fella's doing, for a million reasons that neither of us could quite understand at the time. I knew it was coming (I'd created a sar-chasm) and I cried the whole way to Baker Street station, where we'd agreed to meet, with my hood up over my head and my hair well placed to try to hide my red eyes and wet nose.

I know that I never enter a relationship lightly. I've never gone into one thinking, *Maybe this won't work out, but it'll be a laugh anyway!* I always walk into a relationship thinking, hoping, that *this* would be the man I will end up with, so when those relationships eventually ended, it was like tearing myself in half. Sure, it hurts like a mother when it ends, but while it lasted I was happier than I ever thought was possible, and I know I can feel that way again with someone else who is better suited to me!

So, even though there is no right way to handle all those feelings when you've broken up with someone/been broken up with, here are a few things I'd recommend *not* doing . . .

ISOLATION

This is unwise because a break-up is exactly the time you need your friends and loved ones around, and a lot of them will *want* to be there for you, so pushing them away often actually makes them unhappier than if you just let them help you! Have a friend who you call instead every time you feel the need to call *him/her*. That way you're not dealing with the harder parts of the break-up alone, and you're not making the break-up any worse with unnecessary phone calls either. (But make sure said friend knows they're your designated phone buddy. Otherwise they may have a shock when they get a call at 4 a.m. from a crying, howling you!)

REACHING OUT

I'm not good at letting go. (Especially if I'm the one who's been dumped!) So, I usually reach out to the boy who's broken my heart and ask stupid questions like:

"What did I do wrong?"

"Are you sure we can't fix this?"

"WHY WON'T YOU BE MINE?!?!"

When I've been through a break-up, I convince myself that the boy who just broke my heart was "the one"—when the simple fact that he dumped me should really already have proven that he was not! Sometimes, it just doesn't work out between two people and the sooner I accept that, the better, instead of pining after a boy who clearly isn't my Mr. Right.

REVENGE

Sure, relationships sometimes just fizzle out. However, sometimes they end because someone in the duo has done something specific which causes the rift, for example, cheated lied/run over your cat/all of the above! In this case, it's easy to resent the other person for whatever it is they did and to feel like you want them to *pay* for putting you through a lot of misery. Sometimes, one person may not have done anything wrong and the other feels that flare of anger and revenge simply because they were the dumpee and they just weren't ready to be dumped. I once went through a very messy break-up in which I was cheated on . . . several times . . . and I felt like I had every right to go to his flat, gather his belongings into a pile, and set the whole lot on fire—but, let's face it, that would have been a lot of work, and what's the use in wasting time and energy on someone who just isn't worth it anymore? Not to mention that it might have landed me in prison too—so feel that anger, for sure, but don't act on it, because it doesn't do anyone any good!

The thing about break-ups is that they suck. Big time. If they don't, then clearly you didn't care about the relationship all that much to begin with, in which case, it's great that you've broken up. There's no point in being in a relationship you don't care about! But if you *did* care about the relationship, sometimes it's a real nightmare to get through and it feels like the hurt is never going to end. The good thing is, it does. It hurts a little bit less and less every day, and after you've pushed through the initial phase of constantly checking your emails, texts, and voicemail hoping that your beloved has called . . . or the period of time in which you lay in bed for hours and hours wondering what it was you said or did that put them off, or when you listen to that one song, *your* song, and sing alone to it alone in your house while wiping snot off your face with your bare hands . . . once you've persevered through all of that, with the help of your close friends who don't mind seeing you in such a snotty, weepy state (and let's face it, sometimes you need to go through those crappy bits before it starts to get better), it gets better! The healing process begins. Every day without them is a day with yourself, and I bet you're pretty darn awesome! It's another day closer

Every day without them is a day with yourself, and I bet you're pretty darn awesome!

to finding someone better suited who doesn't mind that you snore in your sleep, who loves that you snort when you laugh, and who thinks it's cute that you've got slightly wonky ears. (No, I am not talking about myself. Shhhh!) Each day your heart heals a little bit more and the memory of *them* isn't as painful. You get to a point further down the road where you look back and see just how crappy and hard it was back then and how much easier it's become. They say time heals everything, but the problem with that is that it takes time . . . obviously. So you just need to keep waking up and muddling through as best you can!

17

Losing What You Never Had

AS I'VE SAID, I GET ATTACHED TO PEOPLE *SUPER* FAST.

When I decided to end things with my first boyfriend, it took me a long while before I had the courage to voice what I felt. This wasn't because I was scared he'd be hurt—I knew he could look after himself—but because I wasn't just giving up the boy, I was giving up the future I had created and imagined with him as well. It was the two children we'd said we'd have, the cottage just outside of London we'd said we'd live in, the breakfasts in bed he'd said he'd cook me, the desserts I'd said I'd bake him, the dog we wanted to get . . . We'd created this whole life together in our heads—not meant for now, but for when we were older and still together. Even though I knew he wasn't right for me and I'd fallen out of love with him, I still loved the future I thought I could have with him, and it broke my heart to know I was sacrificing it.

I don't think I'm the only one who does this. We all ask our partners questions about what they want for their futures to see how it fits in with our own ideas. We figure out where we'd live, and whether we'd have a dog or a cat, and pick out names for potential children. We rarely enter into relationships thinking they won't work out, and the older you get, the closer those futures seem, so we set off hoping that it will never end and that the future we start to talk about is a sure thing. So if/when it does end, even if we're the ones doing the breaking up and are prepared to lose the person we're with, we're less prepared to lose the future we've become used to dreaming of.

That decision to end it with my first boyfriend was a difficult one. But an idea of a perfect future together isn't ever going to be a reality if you're sure that your present relationship isn't one you want to stay in. Imaginary futures are exactly that: imaginary. We picture things perfectly because we allow ourselves that perfection in our own fantasies—but if we're unsure about the person we're with *now*, that future won't be perfect when we eventually reach it. How can it be, when you've known all along that they just weren't right for you? However, the great thing about imaginary futures is that you can have them with anyone you choose to be with. So let go of that future with the person who you know isn't right for you, and go start creating a new one with someone who just might be!

18

Dating Myself

FOR THE GREATER PART OF 2013, I WAS SINGLE. Single in the sense that I wasn't officially labeled one man's girl. But I am very bad at being entirely unattached. Especially romantically. I don't think I've ever been alone and romantically un-involved for longer than a couple of weeks since I was fifteen. I thought it was because I enjoyed being attached to someone, being part of a team. Now, however, I realize that as much as I enjoy my own company, the reason I'm rarely single is because I physically, mentally, and emotionally don't know how to be on my own. As soon as I'm on my own again, I start seeking out another person to share my life with because being alone is too terrifying.

So, in light of this slightly scary discovery, I carefully and affectionately untied all knots from the dock that was filled with hearts, roses, and the few people that held some kind of affection for me, and I pushed off into the sea in a boat big enough for one: me. I wanted to date myself for a while, and to be quite honest, I was so excited. I was looking forward to discovering the *me* beneath all the influences of those I had been so closely involved with. When we're in a relationship, we sometimes forget the password to the happiness file in our brains and hearts and we get the other person to WeTransfer some of their happiness to us. I realized I had stopped even trying to remember my password, and that meant whenever I wasn't with someone I'd crumble. I'd have no source of happiness because I'd lost my own password and "he" wasn't there to transfer it to me. And instead of trying to find my own reserves, I'd just sit in the dark waiting until I saw him again. So now, I wanted to be entirely me. Completely uninfluenced by previous partners. You know how they say that owners start to look like their dogs after a while? Well, I've noticed that partners tend to do the same too, which is bound to happen when you spend so much time with one person! But now, I wanted to see *my* taste in clothes when I looked in the mirror, not a color combination I picked to match my partner's eyes. I wanted to order olives in a restaurant before my meal because I love them, when formerly I would have turned down the tasty treat as none of my previous boyfriends have liked the taste of them. I wanted to be the purest form of me there was. Not-from-Concentrate Carrie, with extra juicy bits. It had been a very long time since I'd done that, and at the end of my "me party" I was sure I'd be far better equipped to enter into another romantic endeavor knowing exactly who and what I am.

It was *wonderful*. The overall experience of being entirely unattached, entirely free, was so much *fun*. After years of sharing my happiness with another, suddenly it was all mine. I felt like a naughty sibling who refused to share her best chocolate with her brother and guzzled it up quickly, all to herself. The downside was that it meant all my unhappiness was my own too, and I had no immediate person to run to when I turned a darkened corner but, hey, that's what friends

are for! It took a little getting used to and, in all honesty, it didn't last as long as it probably should have, but it was weird to discover that I'd somehow forgotten myself, even though I'm sure I was present all along. I'd forgotten what it was like to make a decision on the spot and not have to turn to the person next to me and ask, "Is that OK with you?" I spent my free time drawing, painting, and reading. It's not that I wasn't allowed to when I was with someone; I'd never date someone so restricting! But when I had someone else in my life that was so important to me, I'd spend my spare hour on the phone with them, or I'd while away many minutes of the day texting them. I'd find some way to be constantly in contact with them, and it was weird not feeling like I *had* to do that. My time was all mine to do with as I wished. It felt kind of unnatural, but thrilling to be a little bit selfish. It's bewildering how often we sacrifice ALL our own little shreds of happiness for someone else's, even though they've never asked that of us, and wouldn't ever want us to do that for them in a million years.

I encourage you all to date yourselves every once in a while. Go for coffee or dinner alone with a notepad or a sketchbook. Get to know yourselves through what you create. Try new things, foods, and drinks, and discover

> The experience of being entirely unattached, entirely free, was so much *fun*. After years of sharing my happiness, suddenly it was all mine.

new likes and dislikes you never knew you had. It'll be like getting to know an entirely new person without the worry of where it's going or if you're moving too fast. You'll be entirely in control of your little boat built for one, and the fun is in getting to know the crew: you.

19

The Idea of Love

"And if that joy, that thrill, doesn't thrill like you think it will."

TRYING TO FIGURE OUT WHETHER I'M IN LOVE with a boy or I'm in love with the idea of the *life* I could live with that boy is difficult, because they're not necessarily the same thing. I have often had crushes that went nowhere. They either fizzle out after a while, or after having gotten to know the guy, when I realize we'd be better as friends. Or it's unrequited love at its finest and when I'm right in the midst of that crush, at the eye of the storm, I create this image in my head of the boy and the relationship we'll have . . . but that image isn't necessarily what it would actually be like to be with him, and it's very hard to figure out what's real and what's not. It's like when Glinda in *Wicked* finally gets Fiyero: By the time she's gotten around to finally getting the "perfect" boy that she's been giddily going on and on about forever, she has a change of heart, *he* has a change of heart, and it isn't at all how she'd imagined it would be. It is actually rather disappointing because that thrill she thought would come with being in the arms of the boy of her dreams doesn't thrill like she thought it . . . would (which sounds better when it rhymes in the song!). It can be hugely disappointing when you've been desperately in love with someone for so long and then, when you finally get what you wanted and you kiss them for the first time or you start a relationship, what you'd built up to be this perfect, beautiful, almost movie-like thing in your head . . . doesn't actually reflect the real-life situation. It happens not just in romance but all manner of situations. When you eventually get the job you've wanted for so long . . . only to find that your boss is a bit of an arse and makes your time at work miserable or the job isn't the challenge you'd thought it'd be. When that dress you've been saving up for finally arrives in the post . . . and it doesn't actually look as good on you as it did on the hanger. SO majorly disappointing.

I've learned over the years to keep telling myself and other people when talking about a current crush "it may not be anything" or "it's just the early days" because it prevents me from getting too ahead of myself, which I have a *huge* tendency to do. I get attached very fast, only to have it go nowhere and end up feeling a little embarrassed at how happy and loved-up I became, and so quickly. But then, should you ever regret feeling happy and loved-up even if it went nowhere? I'm inclined to say no, but it's hard not to feel a little bit silly when you were skipping down a path you thought was going to lead somewhere awesome, only to find out that it was a dead end . . . and not only that, but everyone else around you could see you were walking toward a brick wall! Not that that's EVER happened to me before . . . Nope.

> **Should you ever regret feeling happy?**

Trying to differentiate between being *in love* with the actual person or the *idea* of being with that person is hard. Maybe even impossible. C'mon, I don't have all the answers! But I think it's an interesting thing to think about when you're starting out with someone new or you've developed a new crush on someone. And even if we do get a bit carried away and it turns out to be nothing, that may not necessarily be a bad thing—even if you do feel a bit silly. It's always nice to feel good and giddy, even if it's only short-lived.

ACT 4

The Internet:
It's More Than
Just Lolcatz

20

Internetiquette

OH GOSH, I DON'T KNOW WHERE TO BEGIN! Depending on which day you ask me, the Internet (written with a capital because it feels almost blasphemous not to) is either (a) a wonderful, liberating place where you can connect with long-lost friends, meet new friends, watch and share hilarious videos (*coughs* YouTube.com/Carrie *coughs*) and share your own creative masterpieces, or (b) an absolutely terrifying place full of people with opinions and trolls and cats and fan accounts for celebrities' body parts. So much good stuff, so much bad stuff. Quite frankly, it's all a little overwhelming. But let's be honest, who could live without it these days?

Even though most of us couldn't imagine life without it, the Internet is actually a relatively new thing in our lives and there are very few rules. An "etiquette" for the system hasn't evolved yet. For instance, is it appropriate to reply to a tweet you've not been tagged in? Or should I say an "indirect"? Should you click "dislike" on a video you're not that keen on, even though it wasn't THAT bad? Do I reblog that post on Tumblr that says, if I don't reblog, a girl will appear under my bed and kill me in my sleep (and even though everyone knows it's not true, it still has over a million notes)?

I'm afraid to say I have no definitive rules to give you. It'd be unfair of me to write a list of rules for the Internet when I don't really know what I'm doing on there either! I'd just be another fool saying that *my* way is the *right* way, and I don't want to do that because I'm sure some would argue that the way I use the Internet is entirely wrong. What I *can* do is tell you what my own personal rules for using the Internet are, and you can agree with me or you can think I'm an idiot. I'd prefer the former, but I wouldn't blame you for the latter! Think of them as more like guidelines, Poppet! (And if you didn't get that *Pirates of the Caribbean* reference you can now shut the book and go away. We don't want you here. ;-))

PRIVACY

Remember earlier on in this book when I told you I had "beef" with the term "stalking" when it came to social media? This is why: If you've put something on the Internet, well aware that your account isn't set to private and that other people have the ability to access that information about you or see those pictures or read that status, then IT'S NOT STALKING if someone sees it! It's like saying "hello" in the middle of a room full of people, and then having a go at the person who replies "Hiya!" for "eavesdropping"! It's like if a waitress/waiter has a name tag on, and they give you a dirty look when you call them by their name. It's absolutely crazy. If you've put something on the Internet knowing full well that it's public and anyone has the ability to see it, then they aren't stalking you. You're giving them all the information and then getting annoyed when they know too much about you.

There's no such thing as privacy. Not on the Internet anyway! Unless you have "privated" your accounts—meaning that only the people you accept can see your tweets, posts, comments, whatever—the Internet is public. Anything you write and post is "Googleable." It's saved, archived, shared, screen-capped, retweeted, reblogged, and will stay there forever in some shape or form. So, before you post that angry tweet, distasteful joke, or naked photo for your friends/boyfriend/girlfriend, remember: They will see it, but so will the rest of the world! Think of it this way: You live in a glass house with your friends and family. You go about your everyday business, thinking no one can see you because you're in "the privacy of your own home" . . . but it's not really private when the walls are transparent, is it? Do you really want the local dog walker walking past to look into your Internet house, only to see you dancing to the latest Lady Gaga song in your undies?

People use the Internet for many things. Keeping in touch with friends, posting funny pictures, voicing opinions, standing up for worthy causes—but whatever you use it for, you must remember that it *isn't* private.

ANONYMITY

You may not be private but you *can* be anonymous. You can register accounts using fake names and even have fake photos that people will identify as you . . . but this does not make you a different person. You are still *you*, with the same morals and beliefs as always, and if you wouldn't say something negative to someone in person, there's nothing cool or brave about hiding behind an anonymous account. If you wouldn't say it face to face, then it's clearly not in your nature to say it at all, and you *know*, deep down, what you want to say is hurtful. That's probably why you're hiding.

OPINIONS

Everyone has the right to voice their opinion . . . but that doesn't necessarily mean you *should*. If you have an opinion (I'm mainly talking about negative opinions here, because positive ones rarely do much harm and are generally quite nice to hear) and you know it would hurt someone to hear/read it, is it really that important that you put it out into the world (wide web . . .)? I'm not saying you shouldn't ever express negative opinions, but there's a time and a place and a respectful way in which to voice them. Often people put out negative opinions on the Internet, not as part of a discussion or to start one and welcome other people's thoughts on the subject, but merely as an exercise of the right to voice them. This can be the cause of many an argument, as I will demonstrate in the next chapter, but for now, you know the saying "If you don't have anything nice to say, don't say it at all"? That.

> If you wouldn't say it face to face, then it's clearly not in your nature to say it at all.

THE INTERNET IS NOT THE WHOLE WORLD

I can't even begin to count the hours I've spent on the Internet. The trolls, the haters, the overly knowledgeable fans, the tagging, the indirects, the fandoms, the Lolcatz, the grammar police, the gifs, and the hours upon hours spent clicking on related videos of cute babies or "real" ghosts caught on film. It's a scary place to get sucked into, and sometimes you get so wrapped up in what's going on online, it becomes your whole world. You're encompassed and consumed by it . . . especially if you've got a bit of hate being sent your way. I once got about twenty anonymous hate messages sent to me in one day, and when I obliviously opened up my inbox to reply to some messages and was suddenly barraged with bad language and some very upsetting opinions about the small portion of my personality I'd chosen to share in my YouTube videos, I couldn't help but think, *THE WHOLE WORLD HATES ME! EVERY SINGLE PERSON ON THIS PLANET THINKS I'M SCUM! ROHNOH!!* Obviously, that wasn't the case. They were anonymous, for a start, meaning it could have been the same person who had messaged twenty times. Even in a worst-case scenario, it was twenty individual people, but that's versus the seven *billion* people on this planet and the four *hundred thousand* that were then subscribed to my channel! When put into perspective, it's not even a visible percentage of the planet that thinks you're crap. It's a little fart in a hurricane of people who think you're ace. Also, you've gotta think about how happy you'd be if you'd never seen those messages. You wouldn't care! It's only because it's been cruelly posted under your nose that it upsets you, but ultimately, you wouldn't care enough to specifically seek out the opinions of strangers, would you? So, as hard as it is to ignore people being ass-hats for seemingly no reason, hopefully, after putting it into per-spective, it should be a little easier!

We all need to remember that the Internet is not a true representation of the outside world. It's a weird, slightly skewed parallel universe where people are altered versions of themselves, who say and do things they wouldn't necessarily do in real life. Sometimes, the people we are online are more "us" than IRL, but sometimes we become monsters because we have anonymity and unlimited access to people's personal lives. So, if ever you're feeling like the weight of the Internet is starting to crush your soul a little bit, as I've felt many times before, close the laptop and watch the news or chat to some people face to face, and it'll serve as a reminder that there's so much more to the actual earth than what's shown of it online.

21

Jeez, It's Just My Opinion!

I DON'T HAVE MANY BUGBEARS (that word always conjures up the image of bears made of bugs—let's be clear, I have none of those!) but one of my biggest bugbears is the phrase "It's just my opinion!"

As we all know, the online world is full of opinions. Opposing opinions, similar opinions, ridiculous opinions, negative opinions, positive opinions . . . millions of opinions, and they often get expressed openly without a thought to who will eventually end up reading them. Don't get me wrong, opinions are good. As you're growing up, you start to form your own opinions and it's so exciting for you. I remember listening to what my parents said when we chatted on car journeys and then repeating their opinions on certain matters to people in school, as if they were my own and I was this intelligent, well-informed young lady with wisdom beyond her years. In actual fact, I had not a clue what I was saying! But when I hit about thirteen, I grew personal preferences and an understanding of what made me tick. I knew that I didn't like rap music or R 'n' B. I knew that I loved reading fantasy and adventure novels. I knew that I preferred prawn cocktail over any other flavor of crisp, and I got to tell people these things when the occasion arose! All in all, opinions are amazing because they're what defines us . . . but we forget that what *also* defines us is *how* we express them. That's where it gets a little tricky. Especially when you're expressing a particularly strong opinion that means a lot to you but conflicts with someone else's. It's very easy to be on the defensive and ready for someone to attack it. This is when "it's just my opinion" gets thrown around, and I've found that these four words are often the cause of the argument rather than the actual opinion.

Personally, I think that phrase is valid in only one circumstance . . .

Person A has expressed an opinion in a calm and respectful way (even if it's a negative one). Person B has responded aggressively, disrespecting Person A's right to express their opinion. If Person B is shooting you down for having an opinion that opposes theirs, then you are well within your rights to say something along the lines of: "It's just my opinion, which I have every right to hold and express. There is nothing wrong with us both having opposing opinions and agreeing to disagree. After all, *it's just my opinion*." In an ideal world, Persons A and B will shake hands (physically or figuratively, if it's online), turn on their heels and part ways, happy with their own thoughts and ideas about the world. However, this next example is how I've seen it used time and time again.

Person A expresses an opinion in a calm and respectful way. Person B also expresses their opposing opinion in a calm and respectful way (going well so far, right?). Person A, who was poised and ready for someone to disagree with them (in that oh-so-familiar defense mode) then jumps in with "JEEZ! It was just my opinion!!!" This then causes much confusion because, actually, no one was disrespecting their right to express themselves. All that happened was that Person B shared their differing point of view, but because Person A's opinion is so dear to them, the mere whiff of someone disagreeing with it riles them up to the point of starting an argument over having the right to have that opinion at all. Suddenly, the disagreement becomes about the right to hold opinions, and not actually about the opinion itself.

TL;DR:

@PersonA: I LOVE CATS!
@PersonB: You're a total idiot because DOGS RULE!
@PersonA: It's just my personal opinion! :)

Versus

@PersonA: I LOVE CATS!
@PersonB: Cats are cool but I prefer dogs!
@PersonA: OMG! It was just my opinion! I have a right to express it! Why is that such a problem?!

Ya see the difference?

22

The Twitter-Sphere

ONCE UPON A TIME, when I was fifteen and I first set up my Twitter account, I only followed friends and only my friends followed me. As the nature of my job goes, the follower count very steadily increased over the years and I'm now, at the time of writing this, sitting here with over three hundred thousand people who have chosen to know where I am and what I'm doing when I choose to tweet about it! It's a rather odd notion, and I try not to think about it very much or it freaks me out a bit, but it means that the way I use Twitter now is very different from how I used it when I first set up my profile. Back then I would talk very openly with my friends, not really giving a second thought about who would see it, because surely, if only my friends were following me, no one else would be reading it, right? I wouldn't ever bitch about people, but I'd happily have conversations with friends about *other* friends who didn't use Twitter, and I'd discuss certain lessons and teachers, not even thinking that anyone other than my friends would see it. As my follower count suddenly started getting bigger, it took me a long time to figure out the dos and don'ts of Twitter—usually by trial and error. I would make a mistake, realize it was not, under any circumstances, to be repeated, and add another guideline to the list. I still monu-mentally screw up occasionally because, as Twitter gains more and more profiles every day, I get to communicate with more and more different, unique people who each bring something new to the Twitter table. This can be a wonderful, interesting, and insightful experience, but it also brings with it new pitfalls that I didn't even know existed.

I very much enjoy the closeness Twitter allows me to have with the lovely little audience I've built up over the years, and I really love watching the personalities of each and every person shine through in 140 characters or fewer. Twitter has made me giggle furiously over the smallest of things and led me deeper into the Internet to find things that have truly changed my life. (Namely, The Quiet Place. If you haven't

visited The Quiet Place—www.thequietplaceproject.com—
please, please do so. It's one of my favorite places in the world!)
However, just like with the rest of the Internet, there is no
etiquette that we can all plainly follow. It's anyone's guess at
what is polite and what is considered rude, and sometimes it
causes even the best of us to get into an awful muddle! So,
again, here are my very basic guidelines for using Twitter.

THINK ABOUT WHAT YOUR ACCOUNT IS FOR

Are you using your account purely to connect with friends
and make new ones? Are you using it for social reasons? Or
do you run a Twitter account for your business? Is it because
you have a high-profile job and need to connect with an
audience? Whatever the reason, it dictates the way you interact with your followers and the things that you tweet. You
wouldn't see Brad Pitt arranging dinner dates with anyone
via Twitter! Hordes of screaming girls would turn up at the
restaurant ready to rip his shirt off. What people in the public
eye tweet is designed for their audience and their audience
alone. They also keep their profiles pretty family friendly,
clean of negative opinions and bad language. (Or, at least,
that's what they aim for . . .) Their private lives stay off the
Internet, so that there's a clear difference between what's private and what's public. You also wouldn't catch @Starbucks
tweeting anything negative as it would reflect badly on the
business. However, if you are representing yourself and you're
using Twitter simply to connect with people and your follower count is fairly low, you'll be more liberal when tweeting about your own opinions, thoughts, and feelings because
the repercussions only affect you. So, the choice to tweet
negative things on your own watch is entirely up to you but,

personally, I wouldn't encourage that because who wants to be negative, eh?

IF YOU WANT PRIVACY, PRIVATE YOUR ACCOUNT

Remember what I said in the first chapter of this section? On Twitter, you live in a house made of glass. Everyone can see exactly what you're doing, no matter how private you think you're being. You wouldn't sit on the loo with everyone watching you as they walked past your transparent bathroom, so do not do that online! But there are ways to keep your account firmly locked. You can private your account so that people can request to follow you, but you have the option to deny them that access and only the people you choose to let follow you can see what you're deciding to share. (If you want to keep your account hidden from the prying eyes of the public because you want to say mean things without the people you're talking about seeing it, you probably shouldn't have a Twitter account at all. Go talk to someone in real life. Get your issues off your chest and, for goodness' sake, go get a good bear hug from someone you know. In real life. Away from your computer. Go. NOW!)

DON'T INDIRECT

Imagine two of your mates—let's say they're called Sarah and Michael—are having a conversation out loud, in front of you, and plainly there for you to hear. Sarah says to Michael, "I really hate [insert your name here]." That is essentially what an indirect is. If you're talking about someone without tagging them, you're still indirectly talking *to* them, you're just choosing not to include them in the conversation. If you want to say something to or about someone, just say it to them.

If it's something nice, they'll enjoy hearing it. If it's nasty, why would you want to say it in the first place? But indirecting is the coward's way of saying what you think about someone.

"But if I tweet it without tagging them, they won't be able to see it!"

Er . . . yes they will. Twitter is public! Whatever you say has the potential to be seen by everyone, including the person you're talking about. So, why take that risk? If they are ever curious enough to search their own name, they'll find what you wrote and it won't be their fault if they get hurt or upset by it. It's *your* fault for writing it. So, maybe, if you've got nothing nice to say, don't say it publicly on the Internet where literally millions of people could see it.

DON'T CHECK YOUR INDIRECTS

Or if you do, at least don't reply to them. Checking indirects, even if you're looking for nice things or constructive feedback that people may not have the courage to say to you, is only exposing yourself to the negativity other, less polite people are spouting out into the world. Trust me on this, it'll only make you feel worse about yourself, even if the positive outweighs the negative. Our human nature is to focus on that one bad tweet in the midst of all the happy ones because it sticks out, waving and shouting, "HELLO! LOOK AT ME! I'M DIFFERENT FROM EVERYTHING ELSE ON YOUR SCREEN!" If you do check them because you feel your reasons for checking them are justified, absolutely fine, but fight that urge to reply to the crappy ones. It's just not worth giving someone the satisfaction of knowing they've gotten to you. But I do strongly encourage you to just concentrate on the people nice enough to actually include you in the conversation.

You know what I just said about not checking indirects? Well, I suck at it. I feel I have a justified reason (looking for feedback on each night's performance by searching "Carrie [insert part I'm playing or the title of the latest video I've uploaded]"), but it often exposes me to nasty people who don't have the *cajones* to direct me, so these days, I'd rather not do that. I used to end up stumbling across tweets not intended for me, but still accessible by me because TWITTER IS PUBLIC! *breathes deeply* Sorry. *composes self* Nowadays if I do crack and search my name, and then I see a silly tweet, the tweet in itself doesn't bother me, because I've learned, after many years of mistakes, patience, and practice, not to let it bother me. But I do often get this urge to let the tweeter know I've seen it, at least. Just to show them that their tweets aren't a secret that only they know about. They're not whispering into a cave somewhere in the depths of an unknown land so that only rats will hear. They're shouting from the top of the Empire Cinema in Leicester Square. With a bullhorn. To a packed-out audience below. So occasionally I'll favorite the tweet, or reply to say it's a shame they feel that way but, in spite of that, I hope they have a lovely day. There's no point in getting down about one person's negativity, and I always feel like I need to counteract that negativity with some positivity of my own. The problem with this approach is that "the Internet" often seems to think I am actually really annoyed, and my way of showing it is by being passive aggressive. Because I wasn't able to show by the tone of my voice and the expression on my face that I genuinely did hope they had a good day, it was very easy to assume I was secretly seething behind my computer screen and telling them to have a "lovely day" through gritted teeth. Once a seed like that has been planted online, it's very hard to try and prove it wrong. No matter what I write online now, no matter what I reply, no matter how I intend it, and no matter how much I can prove otherwise, the view is that I am being passive aggressive. So, I've tried to quit Googling or Twitter-searching myself, no matter how much the urge takes hold of me, and on the days that I *do* cave in, I try to resist the urge to reply. It causes far more hassle (and sometimes lasting damage) than it's worth!

EXPECT PEOPLE TO HAVE OPPOSING OPINIONS

I touched on this in the last chapter, but the long and short of it is, if someone disagrees with you, respectfully, it's not because they're trying to pick on you or call you out; they just don't share the same opinion—so don't make them out to be a villain. It's not their fault that they have a different brain than yours. It may be "just your opinion," but it was just their opinion too. (Although, if they were being a prat about it and were actually being nasty about your own valid opinion, by all means, think they're a prat . . . but just don't publicly tell them that or you'll be a bit of a prat as well!)

Twitter can be a confusing place if you take it too seriously. It sometimes gives people a voice who probably shouldn't have a public platform, and if you let yourself get dragged under the waves of the opinions of squillions of people who are all contradicting each other, you may drown! So, keep your head out of the water and just go for a dip every now and then, but always have the intention of getting out and drying off in the sun. And I mean the actual, real-life sun. The one that's outside. In the sky. Remember the sky?

23

How To Call Someone Out

IT'S A BIT OF A RECURRING THEME IN THIS BOOK THAT, guess what, people make mistakes. We say and do stupid stuff, and then we have to deal with other people telling us the effect that stupid stuff has had on them, and how not to do it again. So what a relief it is when someone else is doing the stupid stuff! And after a brief moment of feeling euphoric and relieved that we're not them, we can't resist the temptation to become the person who *tells* them they've done something really stupid. And maybe that's OK, because maybe they need telling. The tricky thing is not becoming a huge arse-face when we tell them. Having a homemade banner that says "I TOLD YOU SO! YOU SCREWED UP! AND EVERYONE THINKS LESS OF YOU BECAUSE OF IT!" in your bag for weeks, ready and waiting for when someone does something they probably shouldn't, is certainly not OK. Just because someone else has been an idiot does not mean you can be an idiot back. It's not a free pass to be horrible with no repercussions. Because there will be repercussions if you also act like a doorknob—for both of you.

While it's important to let people know when they've upset you, or when they've upset other people and it's probably best that they apologize, it's also incredibly important that you do it in a way that doesn't make the situation worse. Calling someone out online, especially, can be incredibly hard and can make an already bad situation a million times worse.

So, these tips are for calling people out in general but also particularly apply to online situations as that's where we interact with a bigger group of people.

IF YOU HAVE THE CHANCE TO DO SOMETHING PRIVATELY INSTEAD OF PUBLICLY, TAKE IT

If something doesn't have to be public, don't make it public. The only reason to tell someone they're doing something wrong publicly is if you (a) have no other way to tell them, in which case you need to be as respectful and as tactful as you possibly can, or in some rare instances, (b) you know you are right, and other people need to know what you know to stay safe. So as long as you're doing it for the greater good, then speaking up is important in those situations. But if you just want to try to make sure everyone else sees someone's error the way you see it . . . that is essentially a personal vendetta which should definitely be kept to yourself. It's unfair to push that on other people!

GIVE THEM THE CHANCE TO EXPLAIN

Do NOT just leap in feet first and tell them they are a bad person, or that you are disappointed in them, or, if they're a well-known person or a celebrity, that they should not be in the public position they're in. First, give them the chance to explain. "I'm sure you didn't mean it this way, but what you said could possibly be construed [insert way it could be construed]. Can you explain what you meant further please?" Give them a chance to explain what they said, so you have more context and more of an understanding of where they are coming from and *why* they said or did . . . whatever it was they said or did. We all make mistakes, phrase things badly, say things clumsily, and can just generally be a bit crap from time to time. That does not mean we are genuinely bad to the bone. If you give someone a chance to explain and they continue to stick to what they said and confirm they did intend it to be harmful and/or hurtful, that's when you're entitled to change your opinion about them.

IF YOU DO CHANGE YOUR OPINION, DO IT QUIETLY

Publicly slating and hating on someone because you disagree with them is never OK, whether that's online or to a group of people you know. Even if someone has been purposely hurtful, that's no excuse to sink to their level. It's fine to disagree with someone, and it's fine to "call them out" by telling them that what they've said or done was hurtful and giving them to chance to explain and/or apologize, but beyond that, there is no need for you to let everyone know exactly what a scumbag you think they are. Think it. Keep it in your head or write it in a diary somewhere. Don't pollute the Internet or your friend groups. If someone asks for your opinion, tell them you aren't a fan but don't go into every single detail of why you think someone's an arse. The more you go into detail, the less people will think of *you*.

IF IT'S NOT YOUR FIGHT, DON'T MAKE IT YOUR FIGHT

There are people squabbling online all the time about serious things like politics, racism, feminism, and much more and there are some not-so-important discussions like whether dogs are better than cats, whether Larry Stylinson is real or not, and whether or not the cake is a lie. If you aren't personally offended by something someone has said and you aren't the person who said something that offended someone, it's best not to pile in with your opinion, no matter how valid you think it is. You'll find more often than not that the more people get involved, the worse a situation becomes. Especially online. If you decide to tweet out your opinion on an argument that doesn't involve you, it alerts your followers to it. Those followers then weigh in, alerting their followers, and so on. Before you know it, a hundred people are arguing over something that might have been quite trivial but which now feels incredibly important to you all. Or worse, it's about something serious, but the person who initially said whatever it was that has caused this chaos said it very innocently, not meaning to hurt anyone. And now look at the mess! The more people become involved, the less likely it is that every single one of them will be as polite as you are. So, if you aren't politely calling someone out nor the person who is being called out, *leave it alone.*

It is important to let people know when they've said something potentially hurtful, but it's even more important that we let them know respectfully and without assuming they knew it would be offensive or unkind when they said it. Unless it's very obvious that it was supposed to be hurtful, it's better to give people the benefit of the doubt before we go accusing them.

24

How to Deal with Being Called Out

WHEN YOU'RE ON THE RECEIVING END OF BEING CALLED OUT, there are certain ways of reacting that can make the whole situation even worse for everyone involved, and can even lessen other people's opinions of you. Not that you should care *too* much about what strangers on the Internet think of you, but when it's within a friend or family situation it can certainly cause a bit of trouble!

IF IT DOESN'T NEED TO BE PUBLIC, DON'T MAKE IT PUBLIC

OK, so sure, we all make silly mistakes but, obviously, the aim is to try not to say anything that you need to be called out on in the first place—and that is exactly what this tip is for!

To avoid any unwanted online stress (or any stress with friends and family) think about whether what you have to say is negative or may upset anyone. Often, online especially, we can't predict what someone will have an issue with. I once mentioned in a video that I prefer to read on train journeys because I don't like staring at my phone and scrolling through my social media profiles for a long time. Someone told me I obviously thought I was better that everyone else because I chose to spend my time reading instead of interacting with friends online, which is just as important as reading, in their opinion. I could never, ever have predicted that reaction! Ever. So sometimes it really is just someone else's problem. However, I know I've tweeted a few things which, had I thought it through more carefully, I would have decided to keep it off the Internet. So, it really is worth giving it a few more minutes' thought! And remember: A conversation between two friends who are talking face to face is only between those two friends. A conversation on a social media site sits there for everyone and anyone to look at.

GAUGE HOW MANY PEOPLE HAVE A PROBLEM

You can't please everyone. That's just life I'm afraid. As much as we want to be everyone's best friend and always say the right thing to the right person at the right time, we just can't. So if you express an opinion publicly, chances are someone will dislike you for it, and they'll probably tell you they dislike you for it. Like I said before, sometimes it's just their problem and you could never have foreseen someone having such a specific issue with what you said, and you'll find it's ONLY them that has a problem. That's one stranger who has a differing opinion and wasn't very nice about it. (If it's a friend, talk to them about it and ask them why they have an issue and see if you can resolve it, together.) However, if suddenly a large group of people are telling you you've said something hurtful, it may be time to reflect on what you said.

BE WILLING TO ELABORATE

During face-to-face conversations with people, it's so easy to ask, "What do you mean by that?," have them explain so you understand better, and move on with the conversation. It's probably not even something you notice happening within the discussion because it's such a commonplace thing. However, on the Internet, it's a very one-sided affair: You cast out a sentence into the online depths and wait until someone bites, if they do. If that sentence causes people to feel unsure or hurt or offended, it's true that not everyone is going to give you the chance to explain whether you meant it the way they read/heard it. But if they *do,* clarify what you meant!

> You can't please everyone.
> That's just life I'm afraid.

IT'S NOT THEIR FAULT

If someone misunderstands the way you meant something, it's not their fault for being sensitive. You may not have meant it the way they've taken it, so you can't be blamed for purposely being hurtful, but it is your fault for not being clearer or not thinking it through before you said it. Like I said, in situations where you are face to face with someone who you know better than the people you know on Twitter, it's a very minor thing for them to ask what you meant and to have it explained—and for the tone of your voice to make it clear that you weren't trying to be offensive. However, online, where absolutely *anyone* can be in the audience, we need to think a little more about what we put out there, because once it's out there, it's out there permanently for far more people—strangers who don't know you or the way you talk, think, act, and so on—to see and read into it however they wish! So don't instantly go blaming someone else because "surely it was obvious what you meant." It's not a huge amount of blame anyone's putting on you; it's just a case of accepting that you could have worded something better and will think more carefully in the future. And if you've hurt anybody's feelings, even if it was an accident, you *must* apologize.

25

Online Versus IRL

WHEN I WAS IN MY TEENS, first experiencing the Internet at its fullest, it often, quite literally, took over my life. I couldn't help but think of it as the *entire* world. As if my computer screen was simply a window to every single person on the earth, every place there was to see, and as if every opportunity I could ever possibly want was accessible via the world wide web. It wasn't until my street's power went down for a few days when I was sixteen that I realized that that is *so* not true. The whole of my street was in darkness, without central heating, electricity, and, more importantly to me, Internet. No access to Twitter, Tumblr, Facebook, and YouTube. I panicked! I really *genuinely* panicked when the little wi-fi symbol in the top right-hand corner of my screen went grey and displayed an exclamation mark rather than all four bars being in glorious, bold black. The power being out also meant that my laptop would only run on the charge it had left, so I had to use its remaining eighty-two percent wisely. I got all flustered and couldn't help but think, *Well, that's it. I've got absolutely nothing else to do. What a waste of a day!* In that moment I couldn't conceive of anything else to do except desperately pester my dad to call the energy company on his mobile to find out how long it would be before the power was up again! It just so happened that when the power went down, I felt like the Internet (or, as it seemed to me, the world) was fighting against me. I can't for the life of me remember what it was that was going on, but I do know one of the main reasons why I felt so agitated when my house was plunged into the Dark Ages was that I was midway through trying to explain why I wasn't an awful person to someone. My case was cut short.

When things get heated online, they get *so* hot you may as well be in the depths of hell, and I remember feeling my entire existence was caving in when a few people got put out with me. Even today, I often have to remind myself that there are seven billion people on this planet. Only three hundred thousand of that seven billion follow me on Twitter, and while three hundred thousand is a huge number in itself, it barely even makes a dent when compared to the entire population of Planet Earth. And how many of those three hundred thousand are actually engaging in each conversation I have on Twitter at a time? Ten? Twenty? Thirty at most? The situation is always far better than I let myself believe, and the only way I've been able to embed that into my brain is by cutting down the amount of time I spend on the Internet. Sure, the fact that I have a pretty hectic job helps, but, at first, I would even spend my train journeys staring at my phone screen, trapped in the social media circuit. Twitter, Tumblr, Facebook, YouTube, REPEAT! There's nothing wrong with connecting with friends and chatting to new people, but there comes a point where you need to lift your head up from your screen, open a window, or go for a walk, leaving all digital devices behind. The real world has far fewer opportunities to bombard you with voices, opinions, and images you may not want to hear or see. The real world has a far slower pace than the feeds of social media and you may interact with fewer people in a day, but the interactions are slower and fuller and they are *there* in front of you.

Sometimes, we need to remind ourselves that our lives don't solely exist online. We aren't digital people. We may be part of a digital community, but that is not the be-all and end-all of our personalities, of us as people. Especially when the way we conduct ourselves online can be so extremely different from the way we live our day-to-day lives off of the web. Sometimes, we need a friendly reminder to shut the computer. To talk to a real, 3D person. To make a cup of tea and read a book. The opinions of strangers on the Internet should not dictate who you are and how you feel, and they most certainly should not consume your life!

I remember when I was reading my Twitter feed during the intermission of *Les Misérables*. I was sitting at my desk, dressed as my favorite fictional character, ten minutes away from singing her solo song in front of one thousand people . . . and a tweet from a stranger telling me they thought I was fat ruined my night. But what does it matter that one person thought that of me when I was literally living out my wildest dream? When things are put into perspective like that, it seems so silly and so simple to shrug off, but when my phone buzzed and that nasty little tweet burst on to my screen, it was so easy to be consumed by it. It was so easy to let my heart sink into my shoes and my cheeks flush with embarrassment and frustration. Having someone tell me to put my phone away and remind me what the more important, overriding situation was—that I was about to go out on stage in front of a big crowd and be Éponine Thénardier—well, it would have helped a great deal.

Now, I don't know your individual situations, but I'm sure you all have something going for you. Whether you see it or not, I *know* you do. Something that makes you unique, special, and *happy*. When the Internet is getting on top of you and it's starting to feel like the walls are caving in, turn off whatever device it is you've got your eyes stuck to and remind yourself of that happy thing. Remind yourself why those strangers online are so wrong about you. Then don't return to that device or the online world for an hour or so. Go and do something that makes you smile. Play guitar. Call a friend. Do something that will clear your mind and remind you that your world is far bigger than you let yourself believe when the Internet has gotten ahold of you.

INTERMISSION

ACT 5

*People:
Imagining Them
Complexly*

26

Onions

DOES ANYONE ELSE LOVE THE MOVIE *MEAN GIRLS*?

What am I talking about? Anyone who's seen that movie loves it. It's genius.

Well, you know that scene where the camera wheels its way around the cafeteria, revealing all the different cliques in the school? Groups of boys and girls who are labeled for liking or doing one specific thing. Math nerds, drama geeks, jocks, wannabes, and the like. Everyone wants to be part of the "greatest people you will ever meet" group, but in reality none of us really fit into any of those groups. Not *really*, anyway.

When I was at school, my year separated itself into cliques, just like most large groups do. I found it really interesting, though, how many of those groups discreetly intersected. There was a posse of girls devoted to causing hassle for the teachers, but one of them was often found hanging out with the girls she took drama classes with and, truth be told, what an actress! The girls who took higher math were always in the common room together, but a couple of them were rather partial to music and could be found sitting at the piano with the choir at lunchtimes—playing anything from piano concertos to pop songs. I was known for singing and acting, but I could also be found playing against other schools on the rounders team when I had the time, and I'm very proud to say I was known as a "big hitter" when I stepped up to the batting plate. The point is, no one is confined to or defined by one specific thing. If we were, we'd all be incredibly boring. The beauty of people, teenagers especially, is, as Shrek brilliantly points out, we're like onions. We have layers upon layers of complicated, wibbly, wobbly, timey-wimey stuff that all comes together wonderfully and complicatedly to create "us" in all our glory. We aren't just one big, smushy lump with "math geek" or "drama nerd" tattooed across our foreheads, destined to be that one thing for ever and always. The same goes for when we get older and get jobs. I may be better known as a singer and an actress, but I also vlog and now I've written a book . . .

> **If we were all defined by one specific thing, we'd all be incredibly boring.**

We may all, technically, get one actual job title when we're all grown up and in the world of business but that doesn't define us as human beings. As people.

On another level, I guess that also goes for the way people act in certain moments. If someone gets angry or loses their temper, that doesn't define them as an angry person. They're not forever walking around fuming, feeling enraged. Even the Hulk, the man who is the icon of rage and anger, is only angry a small portion of the time. The rest of the time he's just Bruce Banner. Normal, calm Bruce Banner. People have bad moments or bad days, or get provoked. The same goes for someone who, for instance, makes a nice, grand gesture for a friend one day. They shouldn't then always be expected to make grand gestures every day, just because they were feeling particularly generous in one moment. We're all ever-changing people. We all go through phases, stages, and emotions in which we change our minds and our moods, so it's dangerous to label someone as one specific thing at any given time. And yet we do this all the time:

Women are bad drivers.

Blondes are bimbos.

Men won't ask for directions.

It's all made-up codswallop, based on lazy stereotypes. Suddenly, we've labeled a whole group of people based on one characteristic, which is scarily unfair. Maybe a few women are bad drivers, but so are some men. It's like if I, alone, shout at an old lady one day and suddenly everyone says that ALL people called Carrie are prone to shouting at old ladies. It's ridiculous. If someone has a bad moment and lashes out, yells, says something they later regret, makes any kind of mistake—it's too late. That's who you are to any onlookers, and that's how you're now defined. Someone who's angry. And nothing else. Someone who's always happy. And nothing else. Someone who's passive aggressive. And nothing else. But we should all *know* that people and emotions don't work that way, because we know *ourselves* well enough to figure that out. I know that I'm not *always* positive. I sometimes have a really defeatist attitude where I just want to throw in the towel on my singing and acting career entirely and apply for an office job. I know that I'm not always sarcastic even though during

arguments I can adopt that sarky tone. I'm a person who's sometimes happy, sometimes sarcastic, sometimes angry, sometimes thoughtless, sometimes thoughtful. We know all this about our own personalities, but when it comes to reading someone else we can judge on one thing and one thing alone, and that's their whole personality, all over, with no room for anything else at all. It seems very unforgiving and very naive to think that we're all like Tinkerbell: Personalities small enough for only one trait at a time.

Judging someone based on just one layer is like picking up a book, reading the seventh word on page 105, and deciding you don't like it based on that word alone. Without context, without all those other words, you're missing the whole story that you may actually love! Without all those other layers you're not judging a person, you're judging one word rather than the whole story.

No one's ever going to completely eradicate prejudice from the world. I'd freaking LOVE it if we could, but it's something that is probably here to stay. I'm choosing *not* to have a part in it, and you can too, if you want. But if you go to call someone a nerd or a geek or fiery or gossipy or passive aggressive, or whatever label you might want to use, wait till you've spent a longer period of time with them to see if what you're pinning them down as is constantly there and not just something that appeared for one moment and was gone the next. Even so, the label you're giving them is only one layer of a whole onion, so maybe peel a few of the other layers back before you give them one overruling, definitive title. People are *people*. Ever changing, complicated, and wonderfully layered.

27

The Right Way

SOMETHING I'VE LEARNED OVER TIME is that when you're unexpectedly thrown into the center of a crisis, there is no "right" way to do things. There are better ways than others that vary from person to person, from situation to situation, but there is no overruling, definite path to take. For instance (*page goes all fuzzy and hazy, accompanied by a tinkling harp noise*) back in 2004 when I was in year seven, I went to Lake Tahoe, California, on a school ski trip (fancy school took us to fancy places!). We were staying in a hotel quite high up in the mountains, and it was like nowhere I'd ever been before. It took all my willpower not to lean out the window every morning, look at the mountainous skyline and sing, "THE HILLS ARE ALIVE WITH THE SOUND OF MUSIC!" I shared a room with five other girls, and by the end of the trip they hated me and my overpowering impulse to turn everything into a musical—even when brushing my teeth, which caused the mirror to be spattered in toothpaste mixed with my saliva every morning. (I also had an unfortunate incident with a bunch of grapes in which I flung my arms out in a desperate attempt to be Julie Andrews: The grapes were launched at high speed across the room in all directions and burst on impact. I left that room very sheepishly, having left grape-juice stains on each and every square inch.)

The scenery was all well and good, but it came with local wildlife—and I'm not just talking about squirrels and butterflies. One evening, a friend and I were walking from our room block to meet everyone in the lobby of the main building to go to dinner. There were a group of year tens walking ahead of us, chatting about things we twelve-year-olds had yet to discover: boys, make-up, and the color hot pink. It had just started to get dark, and after a day of intense skiing (or in my case, intense falling over), we were all pretty exhausted and would have much preferred to stay in our rooms, vegging out in front of the TV, watching American soaps we'd never seen and eating American candy we'd never tasted. So, reluctantly, we trudged in the direction of the lobby, about three minutes' very chilly walk from our rooms.

My friend and I were sloshing our way sleepily through the snowy sludge when a rush of blonde, pink, and Ugg boots zoomed past us, back toward our rooms, yelping as it went. The year tens had sure been spooked by something and couldn't have gotten back through the glass doors of our hotel block any quicker. From there, they turned and pressed their faces up against the glass and watched us with bated breath. *What on earth was that about?* I thought and was about to carry on my merry way when a shadow engulfed me. I turned back to where the sun should have been setting, and standing there on all fours was a giant brown bear, not ten steps away from me (although it was only one big, grizzly leap to him!). I turned to my left to where my friend had been but she'd vanished! I heard a door crash shut and there she was, already the other side of the glass with the year tens. I'd been left alone, and I had not a clue what to do.

What do I know about bears? my mind buzzed. *What is going to save me here? Do I run? No, you aren't supposed to do that, are you? Do I back away slowly? What if he runs toward me?* Before I had a chance to make a decision, Mr. Bear raised himself up on to his hind legs and let out a whine, and that was enough for me. My fight-or-flight instincts kicked in and I chose GET THE HELL OUT OF THERE. I took three steps backwards, my arms outstretched and fingers splayed, as if that was enough to keep the giant bear at bay, and then I bolted as fast as I could, back down the path and through the glass doors to join everyone else. As I turned around to see where the bear was, I saw his big, furry behind disappear into the trees past our room block . . . meaning that as I'd run away, he'd followed me. I'd actually been chased by a bear! Not many people can say they've been chased by a bear. (Yes, I am proud of this epic anecdote!)

Anyway, it was the talk of the evening, but my physics teacher, who was also on the trip for some odd reason, was less than impressed.

"You're not supposed to run away from a bear, Carrie. They think it's a game, chase after you, and there's no way you can outrun a bear."

"But . . . I did. I got through the doors in time. I'm fine, Miss."

"I don't care. You shouldn't have run. That's not the way you should have dealt with it." I would have argued back but to be honest, she terrified me, so I carried on the conversation in my head. *OK, I know that you're not* supposed *to run from a bear, but does it matter how I handled it after everything has already turned out OK? Surely, the only thing that matters is that* I DIDN'T GET EATEN BY A BEAR. *I'm fine, I'm still here, and I still have all my limbs.*

Maybe running away from a bear wasn't the best thing I could have done. Maybe I should have distracted the bear by dropping bits of clothing for it to smell and THEN run away, but I didn't know that was the best way to go about things at the time. Besides, returning to a group of judgmental year tens in my underwear seriously wasn't an option when I was twelve years old, anyway. I would rather have taken my chances with the bear! So, maybe running away wasn't technically the best way to do things, but it still achieved the same result: Me, alive with no missing body parts.

Now, this is an extreme example of a crisis situation that I'd be very surprised if any of you have also experienced. But the same principle applies to other scenarios—some of which are just as traumatic as my bear encounter! Take break-ups, for example. As I've said before, there is no right or wrong way to handle a break-up. Obviously, eating your body weight in chocolate and locking yourself in your room to fester in your own filth for three months probably isn't the most sensible way to deal with things, but if that is what's ultimately going to make you feel better and get you ready to face the world again then *does it really matter?* Everyone has different ways of dealing with different situations because everyone is exactly that: DIFFERENT. So, if you're in a position where a friend is going through a rough time or has a decision to make, it's OK to try to steer them toward the healthier ways to handle things, but don't for a minute think that there's a RIGHT way, and don't judge them for not following your advice. What you're suggesting may have worked for you, but it may not float their boat. If whatever they choose ultimately means that they're going to be well, happy, and back to normal again, even if it takes them a little longer (and what they choose to do doesn't harm them or anyone else, in any way), it shouldn't matter to you how they handle things. As long as they aren't damaging themselves or their emotions, just be there for them—that's what they need. Also, if you are going through a bad patch, don't let anyone make you feel that the decisions you make, that you feel are right, are wrong. As long as those decisions are making you happy and aren't harming you or anyone else, then you go ahead and do it.

28

Journeys

EVERYONE IS ON A JOURNEY AT ANY GIVEN MOMENT IN THEIR LIVES. Some are small missions, like finding chocolate when you crave it, and others are bigger, character-changing journeys that take a lot longer to make: trying to win someone's heart, for instance, or mourning a loved one. Some journeys begin simple and get complicated and loopy en route, and others remain simple or loopy the entire time. There are a million different paths to take and millions of people on different ones all at the same time. But all journeys have one thing in common: They are best understood by the people actually on them.

Our paths may intertwine with others' but they NEVER merge. No matter how close two people are, they will always experience the same situations differently; their paths can become parallel but never exactly the same. No two people live identical lives. We can relate to and empathize with people around us whose journeys are familiar, but we'll never know exactly what they're experiencing. More often, we watch strangers from afar make choices we don't agree with, and we judge them harshly based on . . . what? We judge superficial things like outfits and hairstyles, or deeper things like who dated/married who, or who cheated and why. We do this with acquaintances, friends, celebrities, and people we see walking down the street, and mostly we are judging without any information other than what we see with our eyes. We don't know any of the reasons, motives, or emotions behind their decisions, and we don't know what journey they've been on to get to that point. Yet we decide we do/don't like said person based on the tip of the iceberg and think we are entirely right to do so.

Flip it for a minute. You choose to wear a sweater that a relative, who has recently passed on, gave you because it reminds you of them. It's not the fanciest sweater. The color isn't flattering, it's too big for you, and it's ripped around the edges, but none of that matters because it was from *them*. Now someone, at school say, makes fun of you for it because who would choose to look like that? They don't know that you're aware it's not a fashion statement, nor do they know you're wearing it for sentimental reasons. They don't know the journey you're on, or how far along that path you are, and they're judging you on what they can see, not how you feel. Doesn't seem fair, does it? The two sides of this coin are (a) When you see other people: What is it you're judging? How much information do you really have, and is it fair of you? and (b) If someone's judging you on what they see without knowing your reasons or feelings, depending on how close to you they are, you can either politely explain your reasons for doing so OR leave them to their pointless, false judgments. They don't matter!

29

Living with Yourself

AS AN INTERNET PERSON WITH MORE ONLINE FOLLOWERS than I have real-life friends, I was asked many times if I had a "fan mail" address. The idea that I have fans makes me do that mini-sick thing in my mouth, but people wanted to write to me and I have a bit of a fetish for stationery and post, so I opened a PO box and called it "friend mail." Since it opened, my PO box has become a place for people to pour the contents of their hearts into. I get letters upon letters, pages upon pages of heartfelt words from people seeking advice or comfort. (Or on one occasion I received a letter from a very devout Christian man, detailing the ways in which I was going to hell. Strangely, he never really explained why!) After a while, I started to notice a theme in the letters I received: friendship.

Lots of people who wrote to me were upset about friend groups turning on one member for seemingly no reason that they could see, or the group slowly drifting apart over time. I'm always cautious about how I word my replies because my advice isn't exactly . . . conventional.

Humans crave contact and communication. Without it they drive themselves mad, wondering what they may have done to be excluded and cut off from their friends, family, or colleagues. I know I'm like that, anyway. I can be needy and clingy at the best of times, and I'm often telling myself to "rein it in." It's always hard to deal with being left out, forgotten, and feeling like no one wants you around, but over the last few years or so I've come to realize that spending time alone is highly undervalued. When I was at school and my friend group was going through one of its many funny phases, I'd be a little sad, sure, but I also knew I could go to play piano in the music room for an hour at lunch, or go to the library and read, or get my homework done so I could spend my evenings scrolling through Tumblr. I always got so much done in the time my friends were being weird, or there was an argument going on between two of them that I wasn't a part of! I also found that the more time I spent away from them, the more they missed me and appreciated me when I *was* around. The welcome back was always worth it.

Sometimes, it's nothing to do with you. Sometimes funny phases occur just . . . because! People's moods go up and down like waves, and every once in a while they'll clash and everyone around those people becomes affected. If it's someone else's argument and you're not involved, it's usually best to keep it that way and not take sides. From my experience, that adds to the drama and drags it on for far longer than need be. If they've decided to exclude you, well . . .

When I was in year eight, my friend group was made up of four girls, including myself. Two of us were in one class, two in the other, and we all had extremely different personalities which seemed perfect as we rarely got sick of each other. On one particular day, a day when nothing out of the ordinary was happening with the four of us, the girl from my class and I were walking toward the sports hall when all of a sudden she turned to me and snapped, "Will you stop following me and get your own personality! You're like my shadow!" Well, that told me. We were usually happy in each other's company and I didn't feel I was doing anything different from usual. I had a bit of a cry about it, as any thirteen-year-old would, but then I was forced to choose between moping after my friends for the next few days until they reluctantly decided to let me in again, or I could just . . . get on. Do what I wanted to do—things that I didn't get to do when they were around. So I started using my school library card for once, since none of them really liked reading that much. It was lovely! It wasn't like I didn't want my friends around anymore, but while the group was going through a funny phase, I had things I could do without feeling miserable. I learned to live in my own company without *needing* other people around to keep me entertained. All friend groups go through funny phases. Often, no one provokes them; they just happen, so it's best just to let them. Ride it out and get on with your own life in the meantime.

Finding your own interests outside of spending time with your friends is *so* important.

Finding your own interests outside of spending time with your friends is *so* important, I think. It means that you don't need to rely on your friends as your only source of fun and entertainment, and it means you don't get sick of each other, because you don't all *have* to be together whenever you want to do something fun. It makes you all individuals and standalone people, and I believe that it means your friendships last longer. It's been five years since I left school, and I'm still so close to my two best friends because we all went off and did our own things. We were all so different anyway, even when we spent every day of school together. Vicky Martinelli: extremely smart, didn't enjoy being the center of attention, very quiet and reserved in a group environment, but one on one had a wicked sense of humor and loved to laugh at herself (and me because I always gave her a reason to!). Saffron Manning: athletic, pretty, classy, would do anything for her friends, and loved to party. And finally, me: musical, artsy, enjoyed being able to flit off for a few lunchtimes to sing and paint, but would always come back to my closest friends with lots of new things to say. We were all so different back then and when we left school, Vicky went to university in Wales, Saffron went to university in Nottingham, and I stayed in London to work. We text/Facebook/tweet each other occasionally but it's no big deal because as soon as everyone is home for the holidays it's off to the nearest Italian restaurant for a catch-up. I think the reason we've survived the years outside of school is that it doesn't matter where in the world we are or what we're up to; if we need each other, we're just a call away, and when we all meet up again, we know nothing will have changed between us. Things will have changed in our lives, sure, but the core of our friendship will always be stationary and solid and those changes within our lives . . . whether it be new relationships, new jobs, new courses, new cars, new shoes, new hobbies . . . they all make for great dinner conversation and make us far more interesting to each other! We let each other live our lives, and just knowing that those two are there in my peripheral vision, should I need to reach out for them, is all I need.

Friendships last so much longer when they're made up of individuals who enjoy spending time together, and you allow the relationships to change and develop over time. They often don't work when those people start to rely on each other *too* often for *too* much. Develop who you are as a person. Spend time away from friends every now and again to remind yourself of who you are and what you like, and whenever you next see your friends you'll have new stories to tell them of the solo adventures you've had, so you'll make for a far more interesting friend!

30

Houses

I'M A HUGE FAN OF HARRY POTTER. I've read all the books, seen all the films, been on the studio tour . . . I wouldn't go so far as to say I'm a diehard "Potterhead," but I did sign up for Pottermore and spend far too many hours brewing potions. The main reason I signed up to that website was that I'd heard you could be sorted into one of the four Hogwarts houses by taking a test that had been written by J. K. Rowling herself—it was extremely accurate, and whatever house you were sorted into, you could trust to be right. I answered all the questions and, as it turns out, like Harry, Ron, and Hermione, I am a Gryffindor! But I had always thought I was a Hufflepuff . . .

Over the years, I've realized that we like to put people into many categories, but the two main ones we tend to focus on are "good" and "bad." We tell ourselves that that one person who made us feel crappy years ago is therefore a bad person. That another person who once gave a lot of money to charity is therefore a good person. We find the act that we think defines *good* or *bad* and then label that person accordingly. It makes things simpler in our heads, but boy do we then have an issue when a "good" person does something we'd labeled bad, and, vice versa, when someone we've labeled bad does something undeniably good. It's hard to adjust to the idea that maybe, just maybe, we were wrong. Or not even that we were entirely wrong: Maybe we've labeled someone as bad because what they did was, in fact, bad according to our own morals and beliefs—but we were thinking about people the wrong way.

People are complex things. Thinking of it in Harry Potter terms, there is a part of every Hogwarts house within us. We may be predominantly a Gryffindor, but there are still traits of the other three houses within us, and it's entirely possible that we could act on those traits during our lives. I've called people names before. I've sworn and lied and manipulated people into getting my own way. But it's the fact that I feel remorseful of those things, have apologized profusely for those things, and have learned never to do those things again that makes me mainly a Gryffindor. Of course, it doesn't excuse those bad things I've done at all. But a mistake is defined as an act or a judgment that we later realize was wrong, and if it takes *one* mistake to render us an entirely bad person, just one mistake to make us switch houses and become a Slytherin gone rogue, then every person on this planet would be not just a Slytherin but a Death Eater.

If someone makes mistakes and you decide you don't want them in your life anymore then that's totally your call. There are people in my life who I stopped hanging out with because I felt hurt by their actions and no longer wanted to spend time around them, but there's a difference between someone making mistakes in your presence that lead you to not want to hang out with them, and someone being a truly, all-bad person. Sometimes, it takes years for someone to realize that the way they once behaved was quite crappy, and sometimes it takes even longer for them to apologize. It doesn't mean they're evil. It just means they've got a hell of a lot to learn and, sure, we may not want to be the ones to stick around and teach them, but we need to be willing to understand that maybe one day they will learn. Just because they didn't learn it as fast as we'd have liked, it doesn't mean they are awful human beings. It also doesn't mean that if they *do* finally learn, we *have* to let them back in our lives. It's about understanding that just because they've wronged us, it doesn't forever-and-always make them bad.

Don't get me wrong, there are bad people out there in the world. But I've known people who have treated me and people around me badly because they didn't understand at the time that it wasn't OK to behave that way. It sucks that they had to find out through making the mistakes with me and I had to see them at their worst, but at least I know they're moving on from that experience knowing better and *being* better to other people.

If someone's done something wrong, they can't use the excuse that they didn't understand as a get-out. They've got to say they're sorry for what they've done and demonstrate that they've learned from their mistakes. But the telltale sign that someone isn't an all-evil person is the fact that they've *sincerely* apologized. Someone who was really out to upset you isn't going to apologize for achieving their goal so, if someone's apologizing, chances are they didn't intend to hurt you or they've realized now that the way they treated you wasn't OK, and that's a big leap forward for someone to make. It doesn't mean you have to forgive them. But I think it's nice to see a person better themselves and learn.

It's hard to let go of grudges we hold against people who have hurt us in the past. If someone's making the attempt to right their wrongs and make up for whatever it is they've done, it's still fine if you don't want them in your life because of how they once made you feel, but at least understand that people can change their ways, and their past mistakes don't mean they should suffer an eternity of hell and never find eventual happiness or be given the chance to change for the better. For years I wanted my school nemesis never to find success, happiness, love, or any of the good things in life because of the way she'd treated me when we were teenagers . . . but I feel that shows far more about me then it does her. What sort of person am I if I could wish eternal damnation on someone for tripping me in a hallway when I was thirteen? That's not the sort of person I want to be, and I'm glad I realized that before I bumped into her again at a friend's party two years ago and was more than happy to say hello when our paths crossed.

I'd also hate for someone to want me to burn in hell for the things I did in the past that I now understand were wrong and have apologized for. Can you imagine if every person who you'd ever argued with decided to hate you forever for it? I can tell you now, my mum, dad, brother, cousins, best friends, and previous boyfriends would all have abandoned me. If I'd murdered someone or broken the law or done unspeakable things then, sure,

> **What sort of person am I if I could wish eternal damnation on someone for tripping me in a hallway when I was thirteen?**

I'd understand why they'd want to keep me at arm's length, but the difference is they all know I'm not a bad person, and when they yell back at me *I* also know that *they* aren't evil. We're just seeing each other at our worst and that's what relationships are all about. *For better or worse.*

Even though I've been dubbed a Gryffindor by J. K. Rowling, there are still traces of Slytherin in my personality that are destined to make an appearance on occasion. The same goes for the Hufflepuff and Ravenclaw in me too. But it doesn't make me any less a Gryffindor at heart.

31

Nobody's Perfect

I ONCE HAD A BOYFRIEND WHO I BELIEVED WAS PERFECT. I knew that he burped during conversations, played with his feet to avoid getting out of bed in the morning, and shrugged off blame whenever it was laid upon him . . . but I'd built a ten foot plinth in my head, stood him on top of it, and did all in my power to keep him there and try to make him happy. I sent up food and tea in a little basket on a pulley system. I showered jets of love, chocolate, and flowers through a fireman's hose pointed up at that platform, and I formed a shield for him whenever bad things or bad people tried to climb up and snatch him away from his happy place. And he let me. Of course he did. Anyone would be stupid to turn down a girl willing to constantly shower him with unconditional love and praise. Who in their right mind wouldn't want that? Although, it wasn't like we ever had a conversation where we decided that this was the arrangement.

> Me: *Hey, honey. I'm going to shower you with all the love and affection I can muster.*
>
> Him: *OK!*

Me: *Will you do the same for me?*

Him: *Well . . . not really. That sounds like a lot of effort that I'd rather put into my work right now. SOZ LOL.*

Had we had that conversation, I'm sure I would have backed out far sooner, before my heart had gotten so attached. But as we were going along, it was a pleasure to be that devoted to someone, and I didn't ever notice it wasn't repaid in full. The problem was that I held him to impossibly high standards. Standards that no human can possibly meet. *Perfection.* He was so high up on that plinth that from where I was standing I couldn't see his flaws. So, when he eventually cheated on me, both he and I had further to fall. He tumbled ten feet off my DIY pedestal, and I tumbled into despair.

Now, what we must understand here is that I'm not blaming myself for being cheated on. That was *all* him. But both he and I were at fault in some way in this particular scenario. It was entirely his fault for cheating on me, but my fault lies in believing one singular person could be beyond faults and mistakes. Had I been more sensible and less naive, and realized that this man I'd chosen to be with was just a man and not some impossible god who could never do any wrong, I might have saved myself a lot of heartache.

But this also seems to be the constant battle we have with celebrities. They have what we call "personas," which are essentially the sides of themselves they decide to show us. For example, if you were filmed secretly for a whole week, then on the Sunday you were sent the footage and told to edit it all down into an hour-long episode that would be broadcast on TV to the whole world for millions to watch . . . what would you edit out? The time you helped that sweet old lady across the street? Or that time you farted and blamed the dog? That day you donated $100 to charity? Or the blazing row you had with your friend in the school cafeteria? When you went to that party and looked like a Hollywood movie star? Or all the mornings you woke up and looked like Fozzie Bear crossed with a panda? If you have control over what millions of people see of you, it's only natural to want to highlight your best bits—but it doesn't mean the worst bits disappear entirely. You're still a flawed person who does stupid things occasionally, but you've just chosen to keep those things private for the people you trust more than strangers to see.

I have an audience, some of whom are kind enough to call me their role model, which has always made me feel rather overwhelmed. It's wonderful to know I must be doing *something* right in life to have people look up to me, but at the same time I feel this huge pressure to *never* screw up and to *always* be incredibly perfect when in the public eye, which is rather hard. It comes with a huge responsibility which I'm more than willing to take on, but here's the thing: At no point did I climb up onto a pedestal and shout down to the people below, "I AM YOUR ROLE MODEL!" It's not something I chose for myself, nor do I think it's something you *can* really choose for yourself. If you have a job in the public eye and you're doing something people like and respect, it sort of just . . . happens. But then you're also given this huge responsibility to act the way everyone *expects* you to act for now and ever more and, I've got to be honest, it terrifies me. When I first began making videos, I never in a million years started out that venture with the goal to become idolized by teenagers. I just wanted people to hear my singing, hoping that if the right person was listening it might help me get a job in the theater one day. I knew it was a long shot, but where was the harm in trying, eh? In it to win it and all that jazz. So, the first twenty or so videos I uploaded were just random covers. After I'd started vlogging at the suggestion of other YouTubers I'd become friends with, the idea that I was someone to turn to for advice manifested itself, so I tried to put my own take on it and I made a video called "Honorary Big Sister." It was for a Department of Health campaign to get teenagers talking about subjects they see as taboo or awkward like smoking, drinking, and, the topic I was given, drugs. So I made my video encouraging you guys to use my

210   All I Know Now

Tumblr inbox and either just get some feelings off your chest, knowing someone will read it and that's enough, or to ask me questions that you would ask your big sister. When you're talking to an older sibling, you know they're not perfect and you know they don't have all the answers, but you trust them to be honest with you and not to tell anyone else what you've shared with them, and you know all they can tell you is what they've learned based on their own experiences. That's also what I can offer: just an ear to listen, a shoulder to cry on, and advice based on my own experiences of being a teenager.

Through making that video, I'd hoped that the idea of me being a "big sister" figure would stop the idea of looking up to me as a "role model." Turns out, I definitely can't control the way people think of me, and, for some people, the idea that I'm some kind of perfect human being is here to stay, so I need to accept that and be unbelievably careful every time I make anything of myself public for anyone to see. It's a huge amount of pressure, but I have one half of a bargain to uphold, and I hope anyone reading this or watching my videos can uphold their half too. So, here, in my own handwriting . . .

I solemnly promise to make sure that anything I put out there into the world is carefully thought out and sensitive to those who will see it and I also promise to try my best not to screw up, but if I do, I promise I will properly and sincerely apologise!

Signed,

Carrie Hope Fletcher

Now it's your turn!

I solemnly promise to understand that the people I choose to look up to are first and foremost human beings who will make mistakes on occasion. I promise to think for myself and evaluate said mistakes and either forgive and forget, or move on quietly.

Signed,

_____

ACT 6

I Dreamed a Dream

32

Unrealistic

EVERYONE HAS AN AMBITION. Whether it's one big goal or lots of little ones, everyone has something they aspire to or want to achieve in life. It can be anything from wanting to climb Mount Everest to losing a couple of pounds, but everyone has something.

A lot of the time our goals and aspirations change as we get older and figure out what we're good at and what we're capable of. Annoyingly, sometimes what we're good at leads to jobs that are in a bit of a grey area. The only things I was ever good at in school were music, drama, literature, and art—subjects that lead to job titles like actress, singer, author and artist. Job titles that I was always told were "unrealistic." I think people see those jobs that way for three main reasons:

1. They think that those jobs don't go to just "anyone." You have to come from a well-connected, wealthy background to be noticed.

2. They think that because it's been something they've wanted for ages and it hasn't happened yet, it never will.

3. They don't know how to go about getting jobs like that and therefore think there's some secret club they don't know about, that you need a written invitation before you get cast in films.

Let's dispel some of these silly rumors, shall we?

I can dispel 1 *and* 3 with one simple example: my brother, Tom. He went to a theater school in London on a scholarship but then went to a very ordinary sixth-form college. We don't come from a rich background. Our parents really scrimped and saved to make sure we didn't want for anything and are still working their arses off now. We're not sitting in the lap of luxury like a lot of people think. When my brother was about seventeen, my mum found an advert in the back of *The Stage* newspaper that was asking for guys who could play instruments for a new band being put together by a management company. That was it! Tom went to that audition, and he had no advantage over all the other boys there. He followed an advert that ANYONE could have seen in the back of a paper that ANYONE could have bought. There was no secret invitation or secret club he had to join to get into the audition, and he got into the band (which ended up being Busted and then, through a series of events, Tom ended up creating McFly) on his own musical talent. It was simply because he was *good* at what he did and was willing to put the work in. OK, we can all think of annoying examples of people who've jumped to the front of the queue because of who their dad is, or because they've had loads of advantages in life, but honestly, more often than not, it's sheer talent and hard work that gets you noticed. So the moral of the story is, if you don't try, it's one hundred percent not going to be you, is it? (See Chapter 35, In It to Win It, for more info!)

And with regards to number 2: me. I joined the acting agency connected to Tom's stage school when I was three. At that point I was dead set on being an archaeologist, but after weeks of going into the school offices with my parents to wait for my brother to finish lessons, they asked me if would be interested in acting and I said yes. To be completely honest, the "acting" required for any three-year-old to get a job is standing still and looking cute, saying the odd line here or there, and being able to pout on cue, so the agents weren't going to ask for a monologue from *The Merchant of Venice*. All I needed to do was be cute for the camera, and if you look back at my old home videos, you can see I was a pro at that! Enthusiastic, three-year-old me said, "YA-HUH!" So I started auditioning. I got rejected a bunch of times, and I also got the job a bunch of times. Then at eight years old I got into *Les Misérables*, playing Young Éponine, and I became obsessed with the show. When I left I told everyone that I would be back one day to play older Éponine. As I grew up, I realized how many other girls wanted that role as much as I did and that the competition was going to be pretty fierce. When I was twenty, I got a new agent with the help of a producer I was working with on a musical I'd helped to write (they actually rejected me the first time we met, but then came back to me a few months later and reconsidered after having watched my YouTube videos!). When I first met with them they asked me what roles I'd love to play. I said Éponine and Dr. Who's companion, to which they replied, "Let's start with Éponine!" A few weeks later, I was at an audition for

Les Mis for the second time in my life. After four really nerve-wracking auditions . . . I got the part! I had carried that dream to play Éponine with me for twelve years, and suddenly there I was: singing my heart out, eight times a week, on the stage in London's West End. I can look back and be proud that the answer I gave to the question "What do you want to be when you grow up?" is eventually what I became . . . Éponine. So in response to number 2: Just because it hasn't happened yet, doesn't mean it never will.

No matter what it is you want to do—actress, singer, doctor, lawyer, journalist, astronaut—as long as you're sure it's what *you* want to do, you genuinely think you have the knack for it, and you're willing to put the work in, you have as much chance as anyone else of making that so-called "unrealistic" dream come true.

33

Being Realistic

WHILE BEING TOLD OUR LIFELONG DREAMS ARE "UNREALISTIC" can be a huge damper on our enthusiasm, we also need to be honest with ourselves. Your fantasy of being a singer isn't going to amount to much if you know deep down that you can't hold a tune! Your obsession with being a surgeon won't be much good if the mere sight of blood or vomit makes you pass out cold. Sometimes the jobs and dreams we want to achieve are beyond the strengths and talents that we have. That's not to say that you can't work at it and put in the time and effort to get over whatever it is in your way, but sometimes certain jobs require a natural flair, and if you ain't got it, you ain't got it. And that's OK! If you decide to change those dreams after having wanted them for so long, it doesn't make you a failure. It makes you smart, realistic, and above all honest with yourself.

Me? Like I've said, I originally wanted to be an archaeologist. Mainly because I was obsessed with Indiana Jones. I also had (and still have) a love of history, but as much passion as I had, I was rubbish at it. Scraping together that C in GCSE history was due to some serious cramming. I wasn't naturally good at remembering significant dates and details—I just don't have an academic brain. I have a creative brain, and even though that love and passion for history is still there and I still really want to go on an archaeological dig, I'm more than OK with my chosen, more creative profession. That's not to say what you're good at should come easy. You'll still have to work your socks off but the rewards will be greater.

Being realistic isn't about giving up on your dreams. It's about finding the right one! And don't be fooled into thinking that aspiring to be rich and famous is the only worthwhile dream there is. With TV shows like *America's Got Talent*, *The X Factor*, *So You Think You Can Dance* and all the others, it's drummed into our heads that being famous in the entertainment industry is the best possible career path you could dream of having, that wanting to sing, dance, act, tell jokes, do ventriloquism—any career that involves having an audience watch you is THE dream. It's not. If you dream of being a doctor, that's hugely worthwhile. If you feel you're destined to be an accountant, that's an important dream. If you've dreamed of being a pilot since you were a child and were given your first toy airplane, that's massively worth pursuing. Any dream you have is special and important and worth all the time and effort you are willing to put into it. You don't have to be famous to be successful and it certainly doesn't mean that your dreams are less important, worthwhile, or less likely to happen than other people's. There are people who go on *The X Factor* who don't get any particular joy from singing or

> Being realistic isn't about giving up on your dreams. It's about finding the right one!

whatever talent (or lack of . . .) they're wanting to show off on TV—they've simply gone on the show to get their moment in the spotlight. Maybe back home they're a professional gardener, and an amazing one at that. Or they're their town's best plumber and very proud of it. Being in the spotlight is not *more* worthwhile than any dream you could possess. It's *equally* as worthwhile. If you dream to sing and act and dance and juggle watermelons then DO it. But if you dream of being a lawyer, an accountant, a doctor, a plumber, or any manner of job that isn't in front of thousands of people, don't feel like your desires have short-changed you. Those dreams are just as worthwhile, and it's just as important that you follow them!

34

Dreams Change

AS WE GROW UP, WE FIND DIFFERENT TALENTS AND PASSIONS
starting to emerge, and suddenly we couldn't care less about
what we used to want. I've had many, many dreams and ambitions over the years that I wouldn't say I gave up; I just simply
grew up, I suppose! When I saw Indiana Jones, I wanted to
be an archaeologist. When I was in *Chitty Chitty Bang Bang*,
I wanted to be a toymaker. Then an author. Then a dancer.
Then an astronaut. Then a singer. Then an actress. After some
time spent living with each dream, I realized that certain situations and circumstances rendered my current dream a little
impractical or in some cases impossible (like my dream to
one day be Mrs. Claus . . .). If I had REALLY BADLY wanted
it and thought I was entirely capable of achieving it, then I
would have found a way (I would have found a Mr. Claus in
the world and married him!), but it became less important
over time, and other things in my life took priority as my
own strengths and talents made themselves clearer. It doesn't
make me sad or make me feel like I've failed, because it all
happened without me really noticing. Looking back now, I
see that I never really made the decision to put certain things

on the shelf. They hopped up there themselves when things that suited me better came along.

Someone sent me a letter not long ago asking whether they should be concerned that they didn't have a dream career they'd nurtured since childhood. My answer was "Of course not." The truth is everyone has a childhood dream whether we wanted one or not—but many of us move on and realize that it's not necessarily right for us after all. My good friend Lizzie wanted to be a hoover*. It may not have been a realistic dream, but it was a dream nonetheless, bless her strange little mind. Some of us pick something that we grow to love more and more over the years and strive hard to achieve it. Some people pick a thing that they have a natural flair for, and obtaining it comes fairly easy. Some children pick something because their parents do it and decide later on down the line that it's not for them, and then choose something to which they are far better suited. Then a few of us pick things we'd absolutely love to do, but are plain and simply crap at them no matter how hard we try, so we resign ourselves to finding something we love just as much and are far better at. Let's face it, with my dreadful skills at math and physics and the way I get queasy on long journeys, I was never going to be an astronaut, was I? Many of us don't figure it all out until later on in life. Ricky Gervais was forty years of age when he made *The Office*, which skyrocketed his career. Just because it hasn't happened yet doesn't mean it never will. If you *do* have a childhood dream that you're still adamant you want to reach, and think you can put in the hard work and talent

* I'm still rooting for Lizzie to fulfill her lifelong dream to be a vacuum cleaner, and have written to Dyson to see if we can hurry the process along.

you'll need, then, by all means, you keep fighting for it! However, if you *don't* have a childhood dream, chances are you did have one once, but you've lost interest in it to make room for something else you've yet to discover.

Pursuing dreams can sometimes seem daunting. It feels like you're standing on the edge of a cliff staring at your dream as it sits on a cloud, floating out in the open air, and all you need to do is take that leap to see if you'll fall or if you'll fly. A lot of people don't even try leaping because the risk of falling scares them too much, but to me, personally, the idea of flying excites me too much not to take the risk. If I fall, it just wasn't meant to be, and all I need to do is climb to the edge of the cliff again.

Here are some ways to get you further along the path to reaching your dream cloud!

- Dare to suck. Put your ideas forward no matter how bizarre or bad you think they are. That bad idea could actually be an amazing idea OR it could spark off a brainstorm that results in the perfect idea!
- Be cheeky. Ask questions. Tell people who you are and what you do if you get the chance. Hand out business cards including your email and number. If you find an email address or a number for someone influential that you could speak to, email/call them.
- Don't be afraid to say yes. If someone offers you a job in the field you want to be in, but it's not *exactly* the job you want, say yes and then at least your foot is in the door. You're on the inside and you can climb your way up the ladder or you can wait for a job opening.

35

In It to Win It

OOOH! OOOH! LET ME TELL YOU A JOKE . . .

A man who is in financial difficulty walks into a church and prays to God, "Please let me win the lottery!" A week passes and he doesn't win a single penny. So the next week he goes to a synagogue and prays, "Come on, God. Seriously. I really need this money. My house will be repossessed and I'll have nowhere to live. Please let me win the lottery!" Another week goes by but still he doesn't win. So he goes to a mosque and prays, "This is the last time I'm going to ask now. Please, please help me. My daughter is starving and we're living in my car. Please, please let me win the lottery!" Suddenly, in a flash of light, God appears before him and in a huge booming voice says: "Then please, *please*, BUY A TICKET!"

What with being in showbiz and all, I often get told how lucky I am. And I am! I am very lucky to have a supportive family around me to encourage my singing and acting, to have been given the opportunity to audition for certain roles, and to have met people who have been helpful and won-derful to me along the way. However, I'm a believer that luck doesn't just materialize for those who were born under the right star on the right night of the year. It's not a fairy spell put on certain people who then just *have* luck no matter what they say and do. There is a kind of luck that no one can explain, like how some of us find money on the floor or happen to be the 107th caller on a radio show and win tickets to a concert when they were only calling up to request a song, but I believe that we make most of the luck in our lives for ourselves.

When I was a young 'un, my mum would enter every competition available for kids' toys and DVDs and whatnot, under my name. There was always something turning up in the post for me or my brother because our dear mum had entered

> I believe that we make most of the luck in our lives for ourselves.

prize draws or answered questions correctly on every website, magazine, and newspaper she could find. As I've grown up, my mum has passed down to me her "in it to win it" nature, and I'm still always entering competitions—for books mainly. It's a lovely feeling when a prize turns up on your doorstep, unexpectedly. I once won a £25 book token just for saying what my favorite book was on a newspaper's website, and it was an absolute delight when it got sent to me through the post. But a friend of mine was constantly complaining that I was the "lucky one," always winning things that she wasn't . . . yet she never once signed her name up for the same competitions and it always baffled me. How did she expect to win competitions that she never actually entered? I hear the same sorts of people talking to their televisions while watching *The X Factor* saying, "Why is it never me?" Erm, because you didn't audition? It will never be you if you don't *let* it be you.

Sometimes people are walking along the street and find a $50 bill on the floor. The fact that they were walking down that street, at that time, on that day . . . that's luck. But the people who win competitions or who have seemingly glitzy, glamorous careers that you'd love to have are not as "lucky" as you think they are. Their name didn't just appear in that prize draw with no effort on their part; those actors didn't wake up one morning with a camera crew and director in their living rooms saying, "Are you ready to roll, Mr. Cruise?" and those singers did not just suddenly hear themselves on the radio singing that week's chart-topper thinking, *That sounds an awful lot like me! How funny!* They spent years shouting, "OVER HERE! PICK ME! I'M THE ONE YOU WANT!" and eventually the right person listened.

If you don't feel like a particularly lucky person, stop waiting for it to just happen. It won't fall from the sky into your lap. You have to actively go out and look for it yourself. You'll start to feel an awful lot luckier when you're seeking it out and more and more "lucky" things start to happen. One of the main pieces of advice that I give anyone who's sweet enough to ask me for acting/singing tips is something I was told when I was younger and never forgot: Be cheeky. The "industry" is a cutthroat business, and unfortunately not everyone is going to be as polite as you are, and it's the people that force themselves in front of important people that get seen. Obviously, there's never any excuse to be rude or mean to *anyone*, but there's no harm in giving your business card to someone influential when you meet them. There's nothing wrong with sending your headshots and CVs to agencies and record labels, or to the higher-ups of whatever line of work you want to be in, even if they didn't ask for it. They're not going to find you on their own.

I've always had the dream of being the Doctor's companion in *Doctor Who*. (As I write this, I'm sitting on a train into central London with my laptop balanced on my TARDIS bag.) So I wrote to the writers and casting directors of the show with my picture and current CV in the envelope. That envelope was received by those writers' agents, who opened the letter, and based on everything in that envelope, they signed me to their agency! That wasn't even my intention, and even though I didn't get to audition for *Doctor Who*, I walked out of that endeavor with an acting agent. Some people say that's luck, but it didn't just happen. It came from "buying a ticket," when I sent them that letter.

Your name will never be called if you haven't written it down on that list. You won't be picked to play the next hero/ heroine of the latest Hollywood blockbuster if you don't turn up to the casting call, and you most certainly will not win the lottery if you don't buy a ticket.

36

Possibilities

LIFE HAS AN ENDLESS AMOUNT OF POSSIBILITIES. From the flavor of ice cream we have for dessert, to our choice of career, to the person we decide to spend our life with. Quite honestly, as a girl (and I stress GIRL) of merely twenty-two years at the time of writing this, the sheer plethora of choices I will inevitably have to make sometimes makes me want to weep. Thinking about the rest of our potentially enormous lives laid out in front of us is undoubtedly terrifying, and baby steps need to be taken toward this seemingly treacherous path full of snares and booby traps.

I often get messages from people of the younger persuasion, even as young as fourteen, in a panic that the choices they are about to make will dictate the rest of their working lives. As if their future job depends solely on their college major, which depends on the APs and subject SATs they'll take in high school, which depends where they GO to high school and what they study there . . . well, you get the idea. If you're around that age and you're reading this, please don't worry. No one is expecting you to know what you want to do for the next forty years of your lives. The next few years are designed for you to explore your strengths, weaknesses, passions, and hatreds, and by the time you get to college, you'll probably have a good idea of what they are, and you'll be better equipped to deal with the question: "So, what do you want to do with your life?" But I *do* know how you're feeling. No matter what decision it is we have to make, we all act like our lives have been handed to us like a baby that mustn't be dropped on its head, and the more we inwardly scream "DON'T DROP IT! DON'T DROP IT!" the more likely it is that we will.

As a teenager and even as a child, I was an insufferable, independent little spitfire who just had to do everything for herself, doomed to never be taken seriously. Through the eyes of all those older than me, however, I was just like every other teenager: screaming to be treated like a grown-up and ignored because I was screaming.

Now that I'm technically and legally classified as an adult, I'd be more than happy to travel back in time to when I was thirteen, stop screaming, and actually pay attention, listen, and ask for help. Marriage, children, mortgages, bills, jobs . . . I'd be better equipped to deal with them all. However, as much as making big life decisions makes me quake in my slipper socks (because clearly I'm still in bed, under the covers, cowering from the cold, cruel, possibility-filled world), if the power of free will and decision-making was taken away from me, I'd start to suffocate. I like knowing I have possibilities and feeling "trapped" is something I've not dealt with well in the past—mainly in relationships and my career.

There's an awful standstill we sometimes reach where we look at our futures and realize that our past decisions have fixed us on one path, and we have to ask ourselves if we're happy traveling down that road. Usually, if you even have to *ask* yourself if you're happy, deep down you already know something is wrong, because when you're genuinely happy, you skip through life like a cartoon, not questioning whether you're happy because *clearly* you are. It's not always easy to change the path you're on, but as soon as you realize you're not happy where you currently are, it's *so* worth putting in that extra effort to carve yourself a new road. It's like that scene in *The Time Traveler's Wife* when Henry proposes to Clare and she says no. Just as you see his face fall and his heart sink, she quickly says yes and that she only said no because "she needed to know that she could." Clare needed to know that saying no was always an option and she was able to take it, even though she didn't want to. I feel very much like that. I like to know that *all* the options are there to take whether I want them or not.

> As soon as you realize you're not happy where you are, it's *so* worth putting in that extra effort to carve yourself a new road.

My career came to a standstill back in 2011 when I kept being told to wait. Opportunities arose but I was told to turn them down because the project I was working on (which had stalled) was about to move forward. I got fed up of watching possibilities pass me by while being chained up and not having any choice about whether I could grab them or not. I still feel I'm not quite ready to pick one career, one future to live with forever.

So, to those of you panicking about your course selections, if *I'm* too young to figure out what that *one* future is for me, so are you! Just do the best you can to find a direction to head in, and that's all anyone can ask of you.

ACT 7

Turning That Frown Upside Down

37

Nice for No Reason

THE IDEA OF BEING "NICE FOR NO REASON" is something I've talked about a lot in my videos, but I've only ever encountered it a handful of times in my life. I think, these days, it's seen as "uncool" to show any kind of helpfulness or sincerity to strangers. Especially when you're a teenager. You're called a teacher's pet if you give one of your instructors a hand with some books or if you run an errand for them. Why would you possibly take time out of your day to do something for someone else when you will, quite clearly, get nothing out of it? This is the question I was asked after I stopped to give a rather lost-looking man some help with directions, even though he didn't ask. My answer is: "Why do I need a reason?" I don't want this chapter to sound like it should be called "Here's Carrie the Saint Preaching Why She's Better Than Everyone Else" because, honestly, I never used to be like this. It's only in recent years that I've discovered what random acts of kindness can do for a person's day, or even for a person's outlook on life in general.

For instance, I used to go to this little café behind the theater for lunch before a show. The staff in there were always nice, but the busy, bustling, working lunch-hour customers weren't prone to a bit of friendly chatter while buying their food. They'd rush in, grab the nearest bread-based, plastic-wrapped package, throw money on the counter, and rush back out again, tearing at the plastic with their teeth on the way. I always used to get into London horrendously early, which meant I had more time to buy my food, eat it, and probably even enough time to get the train home and back again. So I'd peruse the café's food options for a good long while, make my choice, change my mind twice over, and then pick up three or four impulse buys at the counter like chocolate and popcorn bars while chatting away to the staff. Over time, the staff members took to calling me Julia because one of them thought I looked like Julia Roberts, and as much as I didn't see the resemblance I certainly wasn't going to turn away that compliment. "Hi, Julia!" they'd call over the heads of the twenty people in line in front of me, and I'd wave my hand—usually holding a sandwich—back at them.

After a couple of months, I started to get a little sick of soup and sandwiches, so I tried a few other eateries in the area. When I returned to this café after a couple of weeks of not seeing them all, one of the lovely men behind the counter—who I always called by his name as it was on the little badge pinned to his shirt and it felt rude not to—offered me a coffee, on the house. I protested as I felt I hadn't done anything to deserve one, and he simply batted away my protests and called out, "One mocha!" to the man at the coffee machine, and looked at me in an "it's outta my hands" kind of way. I thanked him a hundred times over for his kindness and all he said in return was, "It's not often someone comes in who makes the effort to treat us like humans," and he handed me the mocha and sent me on my way.

Once in the theater, I was full of glee, telling my colleagues that the lovely man in the café had given me a free coffee. Everyone started telling me how "lucky" I was and complaining *they* never got free stuff.

"They must know you work at the theater and are trying to get free promotion."

"They must know how many Twitter followers you have. They're clever in that café."

"He probably fancies you and wants a date!"

Not once had I mentioned where I worked or what I did to anyone in that café, and never had they asked me. It was simply a case of mutual human kindness. It wasn't the lucky star I was born under working its magic, nor was it a fairy waving her wand and putting me under a luck spell. It was people responding to kindness with kindness. It's not like the other customers, who had tight schedules to keep to and desks to return to, were doing anything wrong by not stopping to chat. But seeing as I had the time, why not have a natter with some bored staff members who wanted to be nattered at?

I never used to be like that. I used to be far more shy than I am now, so talking to the people at the cash registers never felt comfortable. I wouldn't even say "bless you" to a stranger who sneezed on public transport. All my common courtesy went out the window because I didn't want them thinking I was flirting, a little odd, or over friendly. I had a whole list of things I didn't want to be seen as. Don't get me wrong, I'm still on board with "stranger danger." Don't go taking sweets from strangers or asking random people back to your flat. But remember that not everyone is a bad person and not everyone is out to kidnap you. What are the odds that every individual man/woman who sat next to you on every train you've ever taken was a serial killer? Pretty unlikely! It's OK to say "bless you" to someone who sneezes, even if they're not used to that and look at you like you just shot a puppy and laid it in their laps. It's all right to stop and give someone directions when they walk up to you and ask you in the street—although, it's just good common sense to keep a firm grip on your bag or your hand on your phone in your pocket.

Being nice to the people around you, even if you're not their best friend and they're just a stranger in the same train carriage, *makes you luckier*. I'm not saying be nice to people because you might get free stuff. That's being nice for the wrong reason rather than no reason at all. Be nice just . . . because! It doesn't cost you anything, it makes you feel better about yourself, it makes other people feel happier, and it's such a huge reward when someone returns it.

38

You Get What You Give

HAS ANYONE EVER SMILED AT YOU and you've suddenly found yourself smiling back, even though you weren't in a very good mood that day?

I'm a big believer in positivity breeding positivity. Good karma. That kind of thing. Vice versa with bad karma and people getting their comeuppance when they intentionally do wrong. My teachers were always saying this to me about my "nemesis" at school.

"Don't worry. She'll get her comeuppance!"

WHEN?! I wanted to scream. Then she got her finger stuck in the bolt hole of a chair and we had to call the matron to get the Vaseline. I almost died laughing from lack of air. The memory of it still makes me laugh in the same way, even today.

You only have to watch the evening news to realize that there's already a lot of crap in the world. I've never understood why anyone would want to add to that. Negativity and hate are like pollution. Every time you spout out something unnecessarily aggressive or mean, it gets remembered by those who hear it, and it pollutes their once clear judgment of you. You're no longer "sweet Sally," you're "Sally who said that really mean thing that time."

People don't often forget the bad stuff. It's human nature, unfortunately. When someone upsets us or is negative toward us, it sticks out like a red, sore, angry, throbbing thumb and it's harder to forget. But even in the darkest of circumstances, it's *so* worth seeking out those glimpses of light wherever you can. However, if you're the one spreading the negativity in the first place, your friends, family, colleagues, or nosy eavesdroppers on public transport will remember your negativity and it will, most likely, pollute their idea of you—and their mood.

What you put into the world leaves an invisible mark and, although you may not be able to see it, it's present in what someone else says when asked, "So what do you think of [insert your name here]?" or, "I'm thinking of promoting [insert your name here] . . . Are they good enough?" Everything you do adds up to who you are, so why make it negative? There will always be arseholes in life that want to watch you and the world burn, no matter how utterly wonderful you are to them, but this isn't a case of "If you can't beat 'em, join 'em!" If you can't beat them, leave the grumposaurs to their silly little lives filled with nothing but animosity and be happy in the knowledge that you are a bigger and better person. Your kindness will be rewarded elsewhere!

> Everything you do adds up to who you are.

I must add, however, don't *expect* your kindness to be rewarded, or you'll end up sorely disappointed. I once had a friend . . . let's call him Colin! My friend Colin was one of my closest friends when I was *sings* "sixteen-going-on-seventeen" but he was a little . . . oblivious to anything outside of his own life. He wasn't self-centered, so much. Just *oblivious* to the things his friends did for him. For instance, on his eighteenth birthday I bought him a book, a scarf, and a humongous balloon. The book meant a lot to me and it reminded me of our friendship, so I'd spent ages writing out a big meaningful inscription for him. The scarf was because his birthday was in October and winter was on its way, and the balloon was actually from my parents who rather liked Colin and hoped we'd end up together. Colin took the presents but seemed less than impressed and I barely merited a thank-you from him, even though I'd taken time out of the day I was supposed to be spending with my family to see him. Also, when it came to *my* birthday, he turned up an hour and a half late with a card without an envelope that still had the price stuck to it. What annoyed me the most was he thought it was perfectly acceptable to turn up late if he had a good excuse. Which he didn't. "I left late" is not a valid excuse. He and I are friends now but we didn't speak for two years because our friendship was filled with scenarios like that. I was always making an effort with him and not getting the same in return. It's one thing being nice to strangers and not expecting them to return it. They're strangers. You don't know them, they don't know you, and neither of you owes the other anything because why would you . . . you're strangers! However, when you're friends, a level of effort is expected from both of you to keep the friendship balanced. While it's wonderful and important to be nice for no reason and not for your own personal gain, it's unfair to expect your friends to always be there for you if you've got no intentions of being there for them! Vice versa, if you've got friends that you're constantly making an effort with but feel they're oblivious to your kindness and a little inconsiderate toward you, it may be worth having a chat with them! Friendships work both ways and shouldn't be about what the other person can do for you but about supporting *each other*.

Your positivity will, hopefully, make you feel good for having acted kinder to those around you, and it will make your recipient feel better for having encountered a warm-hearted person and, hopefully, a little more inclined to behave the same way toward others. Let that be reward enough, and if someone is nice enough to show you some warmth in return then that's just a bonus!

There *are* genuine reasons to be angry in life. There are terrible things happening in this world, and sometimes it's good to get fired up about them, but use that anger to fuel a change and to inspire others into helping the world be better. Your optimism will start to intoxicate other people too, and that will make for a far better type of people ready to take on the world's problems.

39

Creating Your Own Misery

AS I SAID IN THE LAST CHAPTER, it feels like you can't pick up a paper without reading about some horrible thing happening somewhere in the world. So much of it makes me want to permanently lock my door and hide under my bed for the rest of the little time we apparently have on this earth. Personally, I prefer not to watch the news or read the papers, except for a little gander at the *Metro* on my many train journeys here and there (and that's usually only for a giggle at their cat cartoons). I'm obviously aware of the bad things happening in the world, as I hear about them from my parents and friends, and I'm always signing my name on petitions or giving money to charity to help in any way I can, but I like to hear it little by little rather than in one huge forty-page burst that ends up damp and soggy from my tears. But one thing I've noticed is that, with all that hopelessness and misery happening beyond our control, we're sure good at creating extra unhappiness for ourselves.

There are arguments constantly, day in and day out, about which fandom has the better name, about YouTube adverts taking too long, about which Hogwarts house Harry should have been in, or about having to wait five whole minutes to be served in McDonalds, and I just want to get a bullhorn that can be heard around the world and shout "IT DOESN'T MATTER!" Please, just think about what you're complaining about and compare it to the other truly awful things in the world and then think about whether it's actually worth moaning over and whether you are actually *that* annoyed about it. Is the fact the lift in your building on campus smells slightly like old ladies and cat pee worth the amount of time you spend feeling miserable about it when there's someone on other side of the world who is walking twelve miles every day in blistering heat just to get clean water? Stop creating things to be miserable over when you have lots of stuff to be truly happy about.

I know it's easy to say that you have clothes, food, water, and a roof to live under, so you should be happy because of that—in spite of anything else that's going on in your life. Everyone has their own individual problems and worries that are valid, and it's fine to be upset or down about them. Of course it is. I'm not expecting you to just cheer up because I jolly well said so, but there are a lot of people who are constantly finding something wrong with their perfectly fine lives and making things more difficult for themselves in the process.

I had the honor of visiting Great Ormond Street Hospital a few years back, and I was quite nervous, expecting to leave there in tears at the sight of lots of sad and sick children, but I left in tears for an entirely different reason. There wasn't one room that I entered where I wasn't greeted with a smile and a big hello. One boy launched into a conversation about his love for *Doctor Who*, if it wasn't already obvious from his TARDIS bedsheets and the sonic screwdriver he was wielding. Another girl was sat watching *The X Factor* and was so interested in who we thought would win and told us she was going to be on the show one day. These children were wired up to big scary machines, surrounded by people in white coats, and they were *happy*. They quite literally *choose* to be happy when they wake up every morning, and it is so inspiring to those of us who don't really have that much to complain about in the first place but are still managing to find *something*.

I have watched heated discussions about whether Johnlock actually exists. I've seen people get angry at infomercials for kitchen knives, saying they could trigger self-harmers and that any advertisements with sharp and pointy objects should be banned from public viewing. I've watched videos of girls who have written songs filled with expletives about why they think social media sucks, and I just get to a point where I can't bear it anymore. Why is everyone angry about everything? I'm getting angry at people getting angry! I feel like I'm living in a world where we've been taught to have an opinion about everything and to express it loudly and publicly and ALL THE TIME, which leads to people finding persnickety little things to whine about—shouting it from the rooftops, causing other people to become miserable, and causing me to wonder why it matters in the first place. Nothing seems to be simple any more. Nothing can be planted in the world without it being torn apart for analysis and handed back to its owner in tiny little pieces with labels attached to each part describing why it shouldn't have ever existed. We never take something and enjoy it simply for what it is, which is fine to an extent but too often it crosses the line into the sheer masochistic enjoyment of moaning.

Sometimes I find myself in a mood where I feel like everyone's out to get me.

> *That old lady is clearly walking too slowly because she knows I'm late.*

> *You're breathing loudly because you know I'm trying to read.*

> *He's tapping his pencil on his desk because he knows I'm trying to concentrate!*

Here's the thing though: Everyone has bad habits. My bad habits get on other people's nerves and vice versa and often. And when you're in that mood, everyone's annoying habits are a hundred times more noticeable and a hundred times more annoying. We're so blinded by our own bad mood that we forget that the other person is probably totally unaware of what they're doing. Sure, sometimes someone *is* trying to wind you up, but it's usually very clear when that's the case. Let's give them the benefit of the doubt and assume they're blissfully oblivious to their habits that we find unbearable.

You could ask them to quit it and explain how much it annoys you, but that may seem out of the blue, as they don't know they're doing whatever it is they're doing. You wouldn't want to hurt anyone's feelings. The best thing to do is ask yourself . . . does it really matter? Is what they're obliviously doing SO awful that you need to bring it up and disturb the peace? Is it SO bad that you pick up their shoes once in a while or replace the toilet paper when they've finished it off? If you feel it *is* something that needs addressing, then by all means go for it. But keep in mind, if it's not deliberate and they're not aware of it, the bombshell you're about to drop could open up a can of worms. After all, there are probably a lot of annoying habits that *you* have that they have to endure too! All in all, their good qualities clearly outweigh the bad, otherwise you wouldn't be friends with them. Everyone has their flaws, including you, so it's a little unfair to have a go at someone else for theirs if you're not going to acknowledge yours.

There is so much misery in the world that we can't control, so let's not create our own misery to add to the ever-growing masses. There's so much to smile about. You just need to choose to see it.

40

Choosing To Be Happy

I OFTEN GET TOLD I'M A "HAPPY PERSON." As I've already explained, I do try to be positive and outwardly kind to those around me, but of course we never know what goes on behind closed doors. During my childhood, I sadly had to watch both my parents go through nervous breakdowns; my mum then had depression, and when I was older my brother was diagnosed with bipolar disorder. My mum tells me that when I was around fourteen, she was sure I sank into a pit of depression due to quite severe bullying at school and a lack of friends to keep me company. Books were (and still are) where I found solace, and they were all that kept me from sinking and drowning entirely. During that part of my teenage life, I'd go to my room as soon as I got home, and I would only leave to collect my dinner from the kitchen and then take it back upstairs again to my lair. I felt like that was going to be my life forever, and that thought terrified me into crying myself to sleep night after night. It was only when I was sixteen and joined an amateur production of *Les Mis* that I started to climb my way out of that seemingly very deep rut with the help of some amazing people who I still have in my life now. I've felt the waves of depression wash through my household, and even now that I'm older I still feel its dark Dementor-like hands try to reach out for me occasionally.

How any fourteen-year-old could deal with something like depression is beyond me. My mum did try and get me out of the house for walks round the block with our silly Samoyed dog, but only for me to return to my room when I got back home. Looking back at how I was and the way I felt, I'm utterly shocked that I managed to cope with it well enough that I'm not an entirely screwed-up adult. (When I was twenty, I was sure I was bipolar like my brother, but it turned out that a side effect of the contraceptive pill I was on was depression. Brilliant! When you guys are starting to get all close and intimate with your first loves, do your research on contraceptives because boy did I feel like crap for a long, long time.)

Looking back at how I felt as a teen and the way I once looked to outsiders . . . it scares me. Who I once was doesn't, in any way, resemble who I am now, and that's because I've always made a conscious effort not to be *her* again. She was scary. She was angry, hurt, and extremely lost, and lashed out at those around her because of it. I'm not proud of being somebody I'm scared to remember, but in a strange way I'm grateful she existed because it means I'm able to remind myself in my dark days now that I have a choice to make. Either I wallow in the misery I'm feeling and start to push away the people I love . . . or I buck myself up and *force* myself to think positively. It's not easy, by any means, but it's also not impossible: You can do it with simple things like calling a friend, picking up a book, or putting on your favorite song as soon as you feel that wave of sadness start to pull you under. It's almost like those things act as that door Kate Winslet clings to in *Titanic*. They're your raft when the water's a bit nippy! Also, try not to let yourself be alone for too long. The more often you feel like that, the easier it is to isolate yourself and turn down offers to go out and meet friends. Really push yourself to say yes to those offers to socialize and remind yourself that life doesn't have to be lived in solitude and that your friends *do* care. When you're alone and feeling low it's so easy to convince yourself that you deserve to be alone and your friends don't actually care, or that you're not good enough for them. Your own Inner Critic can be cruel sometimes, but your Inner Critic is also entirely wrong.

OK, so you can't *choose* how you feel. I *know* that choosing to feel happy isn't easy. As John Green puts it in his brilliant book *The Fault in Our Stars*, "Pain demands to be felt." It's not like choosing what to wear. You can't pick a T-shirt off the rail that's emblazoned with the word "Happy," put it on, and then that's magically what you are. Obviously, feelings just don't work like that. But you can choose to take steps toward being able to wear that T-shirt one day soon. You can choose to save up your money until you can buy the "Happy" tee and switch it for the "Sad" sweater you're wearing now. I know a lot of people who, when sad, wallow in it. They roll around in that sweater for days and when they're given coins (or chances to be happy) they squander them on buying different versions of the same "Sad" sweater. So, when I say, "I choose to be happy," it doesn't mean that I am then just magically happy. It just means I'm going to take every step I can toward being happier than I currently am. I'm going to choose to put those coins in a jar that is intended for a far brighter T-shirt.

Depression is a scary thing, and it can't always be dealt with alone and without professional help, even when you've got an amazing bunch of friends and a supportive family. If you feel like you're drowning under the crashing waves of sadness, there's a section at the back of this book that has a lot of info about friendly professionals who are always there to help!

41

Not to Worry

SOME PEOPLE INHERIT THINGS FROM THEIR PARENTS like their eyes, hair, height, or knobbly knees. I inherited my mum's tendency to worry. All the time. About almost everything a human could worry about. As a child, I'd express my worry (and, while we're at it, frustration) through crying, and I remember one specific time when I forgot my geography book and burst out crying due to worrying that I'd be in trouble, and I became a laughingstock among my friends when I got to class. My geography teacher couldn't have cared less.

When you do something to an extreme and so intensely, like I do with worrying, there comes a time when you snap. There's not usually a gradual progression of doing it less and less until you eventually stop. You quite literally break and either force yourself to go cold turkey or you change your lifestyle so drastically that what you were doing just doesn't fit into your life any more. For me this moment was when I was twenty, when I'd gotten to a point when everything felt like it was at a standstill and there was literally *nothing* going on that I could worry about. So, when things finally did start moving along again, there was no way I was going to ruin it by worrying! My boyfriend at the time quite wisely told me that worrying about something doesn't change anything about the situation. For instance, there was a party coming up that someone I didn't particularly get on with was also attending but, whether it was going to be awkward to see them or not, there was nothing I could do to change it, and worrying wasn't going to sway fate in either direction. So the best thing to do was to not worry and just enjoy the party and the company of the people I *did* get along with. Worrying serves absolutely no purpose. It just makes you feel *more* uncomfortable and, most of the time, what you're worrying about doesn't need worrying about and turns out to be absolutely fine. (There were so many people at that party that I didn't even run into said person!)

Also, sorry to darken the mood, but things are *definitely* going to go wrong at some point or another in your life. No one's life ever runs smoothly with no rough patches or little bumps and hiccups along the way. (If such a person did exist, I'd like to have tea with them and coax them into telling me their secrets. OR for them to write this book for me as they'd have far better, less flawed advice!) There's no point in worrying because it won't stop bad things from happening or help you avoid them. If you *do* anticipate a scuffle, rather than fret about it obsessively, the best thing you can do is prepare for how to handle it. If you

> No one's life ever runs smoothly with no rough patches along the way. If such a person did exist, I'd like to have tea with them!

have a plan, you won't be thrown off track or caught off guard when it happens. You'll know exactly what to do, deal with it and carry on.

So, the next time you feel yourself getting antsy about something and feel that familiar knot in your stomach tighten, remember that worrying won't change the outcome and you're better off facing your oncoming storms with a saucepan on your head, a wooden spoon as your sword, your neighbor's dog as your trusty steed, and a plan in your noggin!

42

Hurting Yourself

A COUPLE OF YEARS AGO, I was waiting for my train at the station on a winter's day. It was an outside platform, so it was pretty chilly and the metal of the seat was making my bum really cold and I was just desperate for the train to get there so I could warm up a little. I looked along the platform and noticed this boy, around the same age as me I guessed, pacing back and forth. He wasn't wearing a coat, just jeans and a T-shirt, and I thought it was really odd since I was freezing my arse off and I was in several layers. He kept nervously clicking his fingers and hitting one hand against the back of the other and . . . you know that feeling when you just *know* something's up? I had that. Everything in me was focused on that boy, and I couldn't just retreat back into my own little bubble. The sign on the platform started blinking "STAND BACK. TRAIN APPROACHING." The boy stood with one foot behind him and slightly forward, as if he was preparing to jump. Looking back on it now, I could be making it all up. It all seems really hazy and fast in my head, but even if he wasn't about to jump, it doesn't matter because I know I did all I could to stop what I thought was about to happen. If I was wrong, I just looked a bit weird to a stranger and that's fine. I calmly walked up the platform and stood directly in front of him, facing him, looking him in the eyes. His face went from shocked, to confused, to relieved. It was as if he'd been standing there waiting for someone to stop him and show him he wasn't invisible after all. I've only ever told two people that story. I just did what anyone else would have done had they noticed him.

Day in and day out, I read articles, tweets, posts, and messages about teenagers who are self-harming or have committed suicide and it breaks my heart. I've been lucky—I've never lost anyone close to me and, although I've accepted that dying is part of life, I can't imagine what it must be like having a child, sister, brother, niece, or nephew snatched away from you before their time was supposed to come to an end.

We all have different thresholds for the amount of emotional and physical pain we can take, but the plain fact of it is, we shouldn't have to take *any* of it. I talked earlier about how bullies have their own insecurities and that's why they try to draw attention to yours. But when you're faced with a bully and in the center of a bullying scenario, it's so hard to focus on that point. It must be so hard and so lonely when you're in such a dark, dark place that you're actually considering harming yourself. I guess it feels like it's the only option and the only thing that could make you feel, well . . . just *feel*. But if you're someone who's in that place or you know someone who's there, and you happen to be reading this, please know that it's *not* the only way out. It's not the only choice you have. Trust me.

Before I go any further, I just want to say again that I am not a professional (that's if my use of the words *humungous*, *timey-wimey*, and *grumposaur* had you fooled). I don't know the ins and outs of the human psyche, and I don't want anyone looking to me for professional help. That's not what this book is about. I'm just someone who's been in among this kind of thing before, and I've learned a lot of things that I think are worth sharing, just in case it helps *someone*.

Firstly, you are NOT alone. From the amount of messages and news stories I see, you are not the only person who feels this way, which means there's an endless supply of people to speak to. If it's too hard to speak to family and friends and those close to you because you wonder if they'll truly understand, there are anonymous helplines to call where everything is confidential. There are loads of brilliant resources in the Props section at the back of this book. Please use them. If you are seriously struggling or at risk, or you know someone who is, speak to a professional. I try to always be there for anyone who wants to talk, but I am not an expert, and if you're hurting yourself, you need to talk to someone who really knows how to help you.

Secondly, you ARE loved and you WILL be missed. Anyone who is seriously considering suicide or who is self-harming is clearly in a desperate place and is feeling lost and unwanted, so much so that they not only want to erase themselves from the world, but also think that their disappearing won't make a difference. I refuse, point blank *refuse*, to believe that anyone on this earth doesn't have a single person who cares whether they live or die. I just don't believe it's true. For goodness' sake, *I* care! The millions of people that read the papers or watch the news genuinely feel sad when they hear someone has taken their own life. They hope to God their young relatives aren't going through the same experiences, and their hearts break for the parents who have just lost their baby. The family around you will care, mourn, and miss you, even if they don't show it all the time, but it'll be too late to see how much people care when you're gone. So, *talk to them*. Tell them you love them and listen when they say it back. Likewise, if you know someone going through a rough time or suspect someone of self-harming, show them how much you love and care about them. It could make all the difference.

One of the things that strikes me most, though, is how some people don't realize they're self-harming. The phrase "self harm" brings up thoughts of "cutting," but that's only a small portion of it. When you drink excessively to drown your sorrows to the point you throw up and can't see straight and/or, like a girl at my school, ended up being driven to the hospital to have your stomach pumped, you've brought harm to yourself. If you take drugs to feel numb and it becomes an addiction that you can't break, you've self-harmed. When you starve yourself or binge eat to fit the latest fashions, you're pushing your body further than it can go.

We need to start treating ourselves how we deserve to be treated, even if we feel that no one else does so. Prove to the world you ARE worth something by treating yourself with the utmost respect, and hope that other people will follow your example. And even if they don't, at least one person in the world is treating you well: YOU.

ACT 8

Life:
Proud Parents,
Flimsy Fibs,
and
Peaceful Pasts

43

Fibs

BOY, HAVE I TOLD SOME WHOPPERS IN MY TIME. Even though my dear mum expressly told me never to lie. She hates liars. And too right! Lying sucks. I'd love to just leave it at that. "It's best not to lie, guys!" I say as I trot off into the distance, care-free . . . but that would make me a hypocrite, so let me tell you *why* I think lying is stupid, based on my own experiences.

When I was a child, my auntie lived a few streets away with her husband and three children, one of whom, Joanne, was a year younger than me, and we played together most days after school. We even looked quite similar with our bright blonde hair and round faces and told people we were twin sisters. (Now that we're older we only have the usual vague family resemblance!) Most of my childhood memories include Joanne, and I'm so glad because we rarely see each other now that we're boring and have jobs, even though we still live in the same houses only a few streets away.

One afternoon we were playing in her garden—some-thing involving a football, but I'm not sure entirely what game we'd invented around it. Joanne disappeared inside the house to go to the toilet, I think, so I decided to sing loudly and stroll around the garden, pretending I was a

Disney Princess (which I never do now, of course . . .). On my princessy travels around the lawn, which in my head was now my palace grounds, I noticed something glimmering at me from the grass. It was a gorgeous ring that, without even a thought, I popped on my finger and claimed as mine. *It wouldn't be lying in the grass if anybody wanted it.* It never crossed my mind that someone could have dropped it by accident or lost it, so off I went with my newfound treasure.

Joanne returned a few moments later and almost immediately spotted the ring on my finger that hadn't been there before.

"Where did you get that ring?" she demanded.

"I found it."

"Where?"

"At school."

And there it was. Simple as that. Even now as I write this, I can't even begin to tell you why I didn't just say: "Over there in the grass." The ring wasn't sentimental to me. I didn't care about it at all, but as soon as I'd lied I couldn't go back, because then I would have to admit that I'd just lied and nine-year-old me was too scared. Joanne *knew* it was her ring, given to her by her auntie, and ran inside to tell her mum. Her mum told my mum, and at nine years old that was the worst thing in the world. I stuck to my story and kept insisting I'd found it at school, but then Mum dropped the bombshell that she'd have to call my headmistress and turn in the ring so we could find out who the real owner was. My brilliant mum, who knew I'd been lying all along, gave me one last chance to say where I found it and sheepishly I told her the truth. Actually, I told her that I'd found it *in* Joanne's house because, get this, I didn't want her getting into trouble for being so careless with something that obviously held sentimental value to the family. I was sent to bed immediately and my mum rang her sister to resolve the issue. The ring had been left at Joanne's house anyway, seeing as it was quite clear that it was most certainly not mine.

The reason I still remember this event is because it had such a big impact on my life at the time that whenever I think of it, even now, I still feel the same as I did back then. (It's a piece of soul shrapnel. Oh, I haven't told you about that yet? Later. Later.) From that day onward, I knew what kind of impact lying could have. It doesn't sound like much now, but back then, when the words "I'M TELLING" made me all but wet myself with fear, it felt like my whole world would never be the same.

So, what about a white lie? This is a tricky one. When my friend asks me, "Does this dress make me look fat?" and twirls around in a new dress she's bought online that she's hemming and hawing over, do I tell her honestly, yes it does, so she doesn't walk outside in a dress that her bum's hanging out the back of, or do I spare her feelings and lie? Personally, in light of the harrowing childhood lying experience, I prefer telling the truth but *tactfully*. I think the whole "brutal honesty" thing is absolute crap. It's an excuse to be nasty under the guise of being truthful so no one can blame you for cutting someone down.

"I don't think it suits you as well as your other dresses do—why not try those ones on again?" I've not been mean or hurt her feelings, but I've still been honest. It's not as hard as you'd think! It just takes a little more thought and compassion. Think about how you'd like it if you'd asked someone whether you looked fat in a dress and they replied, "Blimey! Yeah! You look like a whale!"

No one likes a liar but there's also no excuse to be "brutally honest." Tact is the key!

44

The Parentals

OUR PARENTS. THE WRINKLIES. THE SENIORS. We love 'em and we hate 'em and we most certainly couldn't live without them, so I thought they deserved their own little section in this book. After all, without *my* parents I would have died under the weight of my own dirty laundry and unwashed plates and mugs by the age of fifteen.

All the way through my childhood, I was convinced there was nothing Dad didn't know and there was nothing Mum couldn't fix. Seriously. All the parents of kids at school were so average and plain; *my* parents were superheroes stood next to them. It was always, "*MY* dad puts little cuddly toys in *my* lunchbox so I'm not lonely. *MY* mum *made* me this Pinocchio outfit from scratch." (A little glimpse into the lame childhood that was all my own . . .). My parents were just better than other people's parents because they were invincible, omniscient, and, most of all, because they were *mine*. And yet, as I grew up, and my own personality developed along with my own thoughts, feelings, and opinions, I started to notice cracks in the foundation of what I thought was the *fact* that my parents were undeniably perfect. Suddenly, I disagreed with something Mum would say and a blazing row would erupt, or I noticed Dad's road rage from time to time. It's not like I suddenly discovered they were bad people. Far from it! I still think my parents are the best parents there ever were, not because I think they're perfect but because they're two *humans*, flaws and all, who belong to me.

Being a parent is a million miles from Easy Street. I know that because being a teenager is a million miles in the other direction from the same destination, and I honestly don't know how my parents are still standing after taking care of me all these years. As a teenager, I never thought about the effort that went into raising a child. It was just a thing that two people did for me who I assumed were experts after having had a practice run with my older brother. It should have been like breathing to them, surely? Obviously, now I see that parents don't get a handbook or maternal and paternal powers endowed upon them when they conceive a child. (The same way you don't get a handbook on how not to be an awful teenager the minute you're thirteen.) They're just two humans, who are as flawed as we eventually turn out to be, running blindly through the dark for eighteen years, hoping that when the light's turned on, the person that is their son or daughter is relatively normal and ready to face the world on their own. And you would think, after that, they could breathe a sigh of relief now that their child can take care of itself, but no! They spend the rest of their lives worrying where you are, what you're doing and if *you've* left *your* iron on. The job of a parent never ends from the moment that kiddie-winkie bursts forth from between its mum's legs and starts screaming bloody murder.

Somehow, we forget this. We forget that, in most cases, our parents *chose* to have us, keep us, clothe us, feed us—we just give them hell in return for the pleasure of being alive. I get that some people are born into sucky families with sucky parents who don't do all the things that parents are supposed to do, who not only don't put cuddly toys in their children's lunchboxes, but don't take care of their very basic needs. I know that's a situation repeated far too often in the world and I really, really wish it wasn't. If you're in that situation, I feel for you, I honestly do.

If you're lucky enough to have good parents, or at least parents who are trying their best, maybe try and cut them some slack? If you spend days of your life moaning about how unfair it is that you can't get a tattoo at the age of fifteen, or how awful your mum is for not giving you $200 for a new dress, or how horrible your dad is for not letting you stay out past 9 pm, perhaps you should think twice about how you're treating your folks. Because if those examples apply to your life, however unfair it feels, your parents are doing it right. We resent our parents for the things they don't let us do, not realizing that they're not doing it to spite us. They're doing it because it's their responsibility not to wreck you. To keep you alive. To not screw you up! And you're lucky to have parents like that; lots of people don't.

One of the most annoying things my parents said to me when I was a teenager was: "We've been there too." During one particular conversation about sex, that sentence conjured up all sorts of images that made me want to spew. But no matter how awkward these conversations are, it's often better to give them a go than ignore important subjects all together.

Communication seems to be strangely underrated these days, as I have said so many times in this book. Not to sound all public-information announcementy, but seriously, one of the worst things we do is *not* talk to our parents about awkward subjects like sex, drugs, alcohol, and smoking. I know how uncomfortable it can be talking to a parent about sex, but sometimes it's *our* problem. You might find that your parents have no qualms about talking to you about it. I say, "Just suck it up and do it." Once the talk is over, you never have to do it again. (Not until you're a parent and you're on tenterhooks hoping your kids turn to you when they need it.)

If your parents *do* have issues talking to you about difficult subjects, that doesn't mean you're on your own. Along with realizing our parents are just people who may not be perfect at everything, comes the realization that maybe sometimes they *can't* be what we need them to be, or they try but they get it *wrong*. You may feel that speaking to your parents about your problems and concerns isn't an option, for completely valid and justified reasons. In that case, there are always other people you can speak to. It might feel easier to speak to someone you don't really know that well rather than someone who knows you *too* well. Sometimes we feel like voicing our concerns to someone who loves us may hurt them, because it may make them feel like they've failed us, or we've failed them, even though that isn't necessarily true. But it's easy to feel like there's less judgment from someone who doesn't know you. I've included a Props section at the back of this book with some useful links, numbers, and addresses to contact should you feel like speaking to your parents isn't an option for any reason. Saying that, don't forget about other people closer to home. Other family members care about you too, be it your siblings, aunties, uncles, grandparents. Or you could speak to your favorite teacher. My school had a special counselor you could book an appointment with on a Thursday who was extremely helpful when I was being bullied. Your friends are also there to listen, and it's nice to speak to them to gain moral support before you speak to an adult.

The upside to knowing that your parents are human and just want the best for you is that it means you have a more understanding relationship with them. The downside is that it becomes very difficult when you get to an age when you feel *you* know what's best for you, but it conflicts with what your parents want. I often get messages on Tumblr asking me for advice and what to do if you want to be a singer/actress/rock star but your parents want you to be a doctor/lawyer/accountant because being a singer/actress/rock star isn't guaranteed or stable. Ultimately, once you turn eighteen, you are, legally, an adult and able to make your own life decisions, and, as much as we want our parents' approval, you can't live the rest of your life according to what they want if it means spending your life unhappy. Talk to them. They may just surprise you and completely understand. If they don't, as much as it sucks, you need to do what makes you happy.

Keep in mind the sort of parent you want to be when you're older and whether you'd want your kids to turn to you when they have questions about the bigger things in life. I know that I'd want my child, son or daughter, to talk to me about anything. Even if they'd got themselves into a little bit of trouble. Inevitably parents might get cross about certain things. They're allowed to because you are a person, an actual human that they made, under their care. If you screw up, they in turn feel like they've screwed up. That's not to say you're never allowed to screw up. Growing up is when you're allowed to go a bit wonky, but the reason they get cross or upset is probably because they feel like they've failed *you*, not because you've shamed or embarrassed them.

Basically, give your parents a break. They're humans. Not robots specifically designed to take care of you. When I had that revelation my relationship with my parents became far, far easier.

45

Soul Shrapnel

IN LIFE, THERE ARE WARS. Some are on huge, worldwide scales but most are closer to home. We fight and battle with friends and foes about things that mean everything to us at the time, but then when we look over our shoulders at the damage already done, they seem insignificant. The cause rarely seems worth the effect.

Our whole lives are riddled with "explosions": wonderful events like proposals, pregnancies, and promotions, and darker moments like arguments, divorces, and deaths. Even simpler things like kind gestures from strangers or stupid things you did as a child. With each explosion, a piece of shrapnel embeds itself in your soul. A trace of that event gets left behind—and I'm not just talking about vague, faint memories; I'm talking about those hard-core, unrelenting memories that still bring about the smells, tastes, and feelings of the exact moment when they were made. Sometimes, these pieces of soul shrapnel serve as strong yet pleasant reminders of days gone by, but some of them go toward creating who we are today and who we will become later.

Much like Lily and Harry Potter, for instance. When Lily died trying to save her son, the love she had for Harry was so strong that the trace it left behind protected her son and prevented him from being killed. Of course, the magical world of our buddy HP is a little (OK . . . a lot) different from ours, and the shrapnel left behind from *our* life experiences probably won't help us when a crazy person tries to impale us with a twig he found in the park that he claims to be the Elder Wand. HOWEVER, it can impact us in a huge way, if only in a *Muggle* way.

There have been moments in my life which impact me in a greater way today than they did years ago. When I turn toward a certain path that is similar to one I've traveled down before, a piece of shrapnel will dig in and will either fill me with a warm and fuzzy feeling that tells me the path ahead is a good one to take, or it jabs a regret-filled balloon that I've hidden away deep in my soul that bursts and floods me with a reminder of who I once was and why I'm not that way today. For want of a better word, I *cringe*.

There's a reason why things from our past stay with us in such a way. I have a vast amount of memories that make me flush red and make me question if I really ever was THAT person. Memories like accidentally spraying a table full of my brother's friends with my mouthful of Ribena because he made me laugh. The image of that crisp white tablecloth spotted with purple splotches mixed with my dribble still makes me squirm in horror. Or the memory of that time I joked about my classmate's body odor, not realizing she was already in the room listening to my every awful word. At times I've been a truly horrid, badly timed, clumsy, unintelligent oaf of a human being, and those little pieces of shrapnel that dig in when history is about to repeat itself serve as a damn good reminder of what I once did wrong and how to avoid it now.

I don't think we will ever reach a time when there are no more explosions. We get to a point when there are *fewer* explosions, but every time we tread unchartered territory in our lives (and let's face it, when are we NOT treading unchartered territory!), when we have no maps to guide us and our flashlights have lost all power, we're bound to step on a few landmines here and there. Luckily, we have family and friends who tread the ground before us, so they do what they can to help us. They shine their own flashlights on the debris they've left behind from their own explosions so that we can tread a little lighter.

Not all explosions are bad. Explosions are merely unprecedented, unexpected events which include all the good stuff too. We *welcome* that kind of shrapnel so that, when it twinges in our souls, we're filled with that glowing feeling that comforts us in our darkest hours and whispers from somewhere inside that our own happiness isn't impossible nor is it entirely lost. It's *those* pieces of shrapnel that frantically twist and turn when you're dealing with a new explosion, trying to show you that things haven't always been this bad, therefore they won't always be this bad.

If we're too scared to move forward and we constantly stick to what we know, we never progress.

By the end of our lives, we're covered in battle scars and riddled with shrapnel and, as scary as that sounds, that's not a bad thing. A life lived in fear is a life half lived, after all, and if we're too scared of moving forward and we constantly stick to what we know, we never progress. Yes, progressing means we run the risk of being hurt, but you're far better off standing at the end of a journey looking back at how far you've come rather than standing stationary at the starting line for years on end, looking longingly into the distance at where you could be.

46

Ripples

I THINK A LOT OF PEOPLE CONFUSE MAKING A MARK with being famous. These days being famous is relatively easy compared to the days when we didn't have TV or the Internet—says Grandma! Nowadays, you upload a video of yourself falling off a table or your nan's teeth falling out of her head, it goes viral, and suddenly your name and face are known worldwide. Yes, that's fame, but no one's false teeth or skill at falling over ever made a real mark or difference on this earth. It hasn't changed lives or made people want to do something with their existence. It's not made anyone think anything other than: *That was funny!*

Making a mark is about saying something new that no one's said before, or saying something old in a new way. It's about saying something you truly believe in, that you really think is going to change the world for the better, with passion and conviction. Making a mark doesn't even have to be on a worldwide scale for it to truly matter. Just because your face isn't on T-shirts or tattooed across someone's left bum cheek, doesn't mean that you haven't made a mark or a difference on the people around you. Doing good deeds, being gener- ous, giving to good causes, smiling more, being happy toward people that may not expect it . . . it all adds up and amounts to a person that people will always remember as the guy/girl who was always happy, giving, kind, and so on. And when I say "people," I mean the people who truly matter. We spend forever searching for the approval of strangers, people on Twitter, YouTube, and Tumblr who we don't actually know, but we often ignore the opinions of the people we should be listening to. How many times have you heard yourself say something along the lines of: "But you HAVE to say that because you're my mum/dad/brother/sister/boyfriend/girl-friend/husband/wife"?

If anything, those are the people who are more likely to be honest! They're the ones who tell you when you have something stuck in your teeth or that your dress is tucked into your undies. Sometimes they even go out of their way to make you feel uncomfortable because you're just THAT close. They're the ones who will hand you a condom in front of your new boyfriend/girlfriend and say, "Have fun you two!" They don't mind making you feel stupid or being completely blunt with you, because they know you're still going to love them because they're family.

I've always thought that everyone is at the center of a ripple. The ring immediately around you is of your family and closest friends. The next ring is of the people you'd call acquaintances or friends of friends, and the rings after that are of strangers (or friends of friends of friends of friends . . .). The point is, the ripples spread outward and carry with them whatever you choose to put in the water. You do something good toward the immediate ring, your family and friends, they'll tell it to their own immediate rings, who will filter that through to their immediate rings, and so on and so forth.

So when those friends of friends of friends finally meet you, they'll say, "OH so you're the person who did that super-cool thing!"

The kind of fame that comes quick and easy isn't usually associated with good things (there are exceptions, of course, but it's not usual). That's the kind of fame that seems exciting and glamorous but ultimately doesn't really bring much happiness or even last that long. Personally, I don't agree with aspiring to be famous for the sake of being famous. I feel that we should all be aiming to do something that makes a difference, something that makes people remember us for a good reason, rather than just becoming a name on people's lips for a day or a week or two for something that doesn't matter. My advice is to aim to be remembered rather than aim to be famous, because being remembered requires effort that lasts long-term. Be remembered for the good you did rather than having fifteen minutes of fame for something that doesn't really matter.

> **We should all be aiming to do something that makes a difference. Be remembered for the good you did.**

47

It's Not All About You

YOU REMEMBER AT THE BEGINNING OF THIS BOOK I wrote about how on your first day of school, everyone's thinking about themselves so you can relax because the pressure is off you . . . well, that swings the other way too. On your first day of something, you're allowed to be a little self-centered. It's *your* big day and you need to be self aware. But remember that no one's going to like it if this behavior carries on past the first week. Your first day may be all about you, but life is not, and sometimes it's easy to forget that everything doesn't revolve around your needs.

One of the things I love about working at the theater is when we get to properly socialize as a cast—as ourselves and not as grubby characters from the French Revolution. I especially love bowling nights, and was pleased when a friend of mine recently mentioned he would be organizing one soon. I told him I'd be away on holiday from the fourth to the sixth, so not to book it around those dates. Two days later, a sign went up on the noticeboard to say that the next bowling night would be the fourth. I was gutted. How could he? I *specifically* said I would be away, so why did he do that to me when he knows how much I love bowling?

"That was the date that worked for the majority of the cast. It's not all about you, Fletcher!" he joked when I asked. Of *course* it's not all about me. He was thinking about the cast as a whole, everyone's holiday dates, and which date the largest amount of people could make. It was just unlucky that it didn't turn out in my favor.

I've often heard people say that the world is conspiring against them when things aren't going their way, and I've always found that very strange. There are seven billion humans on earth, all entirely unique. Some doing good, some doing bad, some just getting on with life, and yet the whole universe put everything it had, all its power and might into . . . making you an hour late for school/stub your toe/get bad grades? Doesn't seem likely, does it?

The things to remember are:

- Excuse my French, but as the saying goes . . . shit happens. It sucks! But the sooner we learn to deal with it, the easier it is to move on.
- Sometimes when we think "the universe is conspiring against us," in reality we're going against ourselves by even thinking that. As I've said before, I'm a big believer in positivity being rewarded by positivity and good karma. The idea doesn't work for everyone but it's always helped me. Thinking positive leads to feeling positive leads to people acting positively toward you. If you're constantly moaning about how "the world is against you," the world will seem to remain against you until you decide to do something about it!

48

Choices

IN THE PAST, I HAVE FOUND MYSELF IN SITUATIONS that have been ongoing for a long time and I decide after careful consideration that it's time for a change of scene, whether that's romantically, professionally, or I was just fed up of the book I was reading! Changing your mind is totally natural, necessary, and *allowed*. However, lots of people say "I don't have a choice" when they're in an unwanted relationship, a sucky job, or doing anything reluctantly and feeling like they aren't able to get out of it. But often we *do* have a choice. It's just that making that choice affects other people and often upsets the life and routine we're so used to, and that notion is terrifying! So we convince ourselves that there is no other way. We become martyrs, really. We sacrifice our own happiness to make other people happier when, in reality, those people care about our happiness too, and don't want to be any part of making us unhappy. And so it all goes round in a miserable loop and we all end up fake-smiling at each other, pretending we're fine, when in fact our souls are shriveling up on the inside.

I hate making other people unhappy or upset, and I try to never do so intentionally, but when I change my mind or decide that something just isn't for me anymore, those decisions *do* often impact other people in my life and sometimes it affects them negatively. Like when a relationship comes to an end. The truth is, there's not much wiggle room when someone decides they want out of a relationship, and a break-up always sucks for both parties, no matter who initiated it. But those decisions have to be made for the sake of everyone's *ultimate* happiness. If you stay with someone for fear of hurting them, you may find yourself, years later, bitter and full of resentment in a relationship that's miserable for you both.

Sometimes, just voicing your discomfort helps, even if nothing is done about it. I've often thought that I wanted to change a certain aspect of my life because something was making me miserable, but after talking about it with friends and family and exploring every option, I've realized the situation I was in was probably the best one for me. Because it once again felt like I was *choosing* the lifestyle I already had, things felt far better and I gained back some of the control I felt I'd lost. I guess that's what it is really. Knowing that we're fully in control of our lives, that the choices we make aren't mistakes, and that we're as happy as we can be.

Sometimes, we *do* have the option to change something that isn't right in our lives. It's just a question of whether we are brave enough to take the leap and change it.

49

"It's Easier Said Than Done!"

WHEN I WAS SIXTEEN I WANTED TO START A BLOG and just write. Then when I was eighteen I wanted to write about my school experiences and everything I'd learned. Now that I'm twenty-two, I'm actually doing it. SIX YEARS. It's taken me over half a decade to actually sit down and do what I wanted to do, and in those six years I kept saying "I really want to write a book!" The natural response from my friends and family was "Write one then!" and I'd always reply,

"It's easier said than done."

Now that I'm actually doing it, I want to jump back in time to every time I said that and punch myself, very hard, in the face. Negative reinforcement. Granted this would have been a very different book if I'd written it at sixteen . . . actually, to be completely honest, it would have been *awful*. But at least I would have done what I'd said I would do, and it would have been a great experience (and probably a great resource!) for me as I write this now. Now, I can't stand it when people say that to me because I know exactly what it really means. It translates as: "I don't really think I can be bothered to put in the work required." I *know* how hard it is to write a book. I *know* how much time and effort it takes to actually sit down and write. But it's a hell of a lot harder to get a book done if you don't ever actually *write*, and the truth is I just couldn't be bothered to put time aside to sit at my laptop and tap away for hours. Instead, I squandered that time on the phone with my boyfriend and sitting at home scrolling through social networking sites. No one had ever said to me that writing a book would be easy, so saying "it's easier said than done" was a get-out. A way to say "I won't have written anything the next time you ask me either, because I'm pretending the reason I'm not writing is that writing a book is a mammoth task, when really I'm too lazy to start or finish anything right now."

If you think about it, EVERYTHING is easier said than done. It takes naff all to breathe out a few words. It's far easier to say "I'm going to switch on the telly" than the effort it takes to walk across the room and switch on the telly. It's a world easier to say "I'm going to make dinner" than it actually is to make dinner. If we all said "it's easier said than done" to everything, it would technically be true but nothing would ever get done! You don't see Usain Bolt looking at the running track, saying, "Oof, trying to be the fastest man alive is easier said than done!" do you? NO! He just went ahead and ran. Very fast! So where does it end if *everything* is literally easier said than done?

> If we all said "it's easier said than done" to everything, it would technically be true but nothing would ever get done!

No one's going to judge you if you say "I just don't think I can put in the time and effort required for what it is I want to do at the moment." That's a perfectly valid reason . . . but only if you have other, actual, proper things that are getting in the way. Procrastinating isn't great if you want to do something that requires a lot of your time, so it's best to get started sooner rather than later and begin with small steps. I used to write songs for half an hour every day. Even if I wanted to carry on longer, I'd make myself stop so that I remained passionate about it and eager to carry on the day after. Write five hundred words a day. Practice piano for an hour a day. Sing scales for the length of time it takes to shower. Just a little bit every day so by the end of a month or a year you're that much closer to your goal than you were when it was "easier said than done."

Think about the real reasons you're telling the world and its neighbor that what your friends or family are suggesting you try is easier said than done.

"Be more tolerant to your little sister."

"Don't rise to that bully's attempts to provoke you."

"Exercise more!"

It's a lot less effort to tell your sister to shut up than to just accept that she's younger and has a lot of learning to do and then help her instead of berating her. It's easier to bite back and retaliate than to ignore a bully or calmly tell them they can take their bullying elsewhere. And I have perfected the art of sitting on my arse eating muffins and various confectionary smeared in peanut butter and Nutella rather than taking the dog for a brisk twenty-minute walk round the corner or doing forty jumping jacks in the living room. We are more than capable of doing what is asked of us or completing the tougher tasks we set ourselves. Of *course* it's easier said than done. No one's telling you anything you set out to do is going to be easy. Very few things worth doing in life are. We all just need to find the courage to get off our bums and make the effort.

50

The Past and Making Peace with It

I'VE NEVER BEEN GOOD AT LETTING GO OF WHAT HAS BEEN. I was close to getting "What if . . . ?" tattooed on my forehead at one point because it was all I could think of when I took a good look at everything I'd ever done that I hated myself for. *What if* I had told that boy I fancied him? *What if* I hadn't tried to steal that ring from my cousin? *What if* I'd never given up dancing? *What if* I just accepted the choices I'd made and became content with the life I have now? Oh, then I'd have some kind of disorder that meant I was no longer human, because "what if syndrome" is something we human beings are *all* prone to, and it can drive us absolutely stark raving loony. Sometimes, it's so hard to accept what we've done—the good, the bad, and the butt-faced ugly—learn from it, and move on. We keep replaying scenarios in our heads in different ways with different dialogue and different outcomes, and it's ridiculous because we don't have a TARDIS. We can't go back in time and alter events to suit ourselves. And if I did have a TARDIS that would mean I'd know the Doctor, so there would be no way I would have had time to write this book. Screw writing! I pick time travel with a devilishly handsome man!

I always think about the past like a massive vault that we don't have the key to. Every moment that passes gets locked in that vault to be untouched and unchanged forever, and that's it. So, what do I want in my vault? How can I make sure that at the end of my life, when my friends and family open up that vault and get to rifle through the memories and stories of when I was alive, that it bursts open in an explosion of glitter, rainbows, and fairy dust? The answer is: I need to recognize that my present becomes my past in the blink of an eye, and I need to not sit on my arse wasting it. I need to actually DO something, and not wait for my future to become my present and just hope that some unknown entity has made it good for me. I need to *make sure* my future is as good as I want it to be, by finding opportunities (or making them), taking them, and seeing them through. It's "easier said than done" of course but, as I've said before, that phrase is a get-out for people who don't want to make the effort to actually get it done. No, it won't be easy, but don't you want to give yourself that extra push and make exciting things happen? Yes, it might all go wrong. There's always that risk. But what if it doesn't? Surely that's worth the risk, isn't it?

At one point, what is now behind us was in front of us. I think of all those moments I spent doing nothing when I could have done *something*—an activity that actually resulted in a product like a painting, a book, or just more knowledge. All those moments I spent scrolling through Tumblr when my

> **Yes, it might all go wrong. There's always that risk. But what if it doesn't? Surely that's worth the risk, isn't it?**

notepad remained untouched and that book I wanted to write never got started. All that time I spent watching reruns of *Friends*, my paintbrush and watercolors abandoned and that masterpiece remaining in my mind. All those clock ticks that passed while I moaned to my friends about that girl on TV who slept with that guy I quite fancy from that band whose music I don't like, while that conversation with that *real* guy I *actually* wanted to give my heart to remained unspoken. If I added up all the time I've wasted procrastinating, fighting off the voice in my brain saying, "Shouldn't you be doing that thing you need to do?" how much would it equal? Days? Weeks? Months? Who knows? What I *do* know is that I don't want to add any more to that number.

Everyone needs downtime, of course, to unwind, but I count that time separately from the time I allot for work. *Relaxing* becomes *procrastinating* when it eats into the time I've allocated to actually *do* that work. And it's fine that I've procrastinated. It was a mistake and, if we've learned anything from this booky-wooky journey we've been on, it's OK to make mistakes as long as we learn how not to make them again. We should make peace with the fact that there are some mistakes in our vaults, but what we need to do now is make sure what goes into them from here on out is so brilliant that it outweighs all the stupid things that are in there now. It's easier to make peace with the past and everything you've done that was a bit stupid, or that didn't turn out how you wanted it to, when you know you're going to strive from now on to change that. To do better. To not waste all that precious time you previously procrastinated away. We're all guilty of it, but very few people actually change it. I *liked* being lazy, and couldn't really be bothered to change my procrastinating ways. But after having performed in eight shows a week for a year where everything I wanted to do—like drawing, seeing my friends and loved ones, and writing this very book—had to go on hold, suddenly those fifteen-minute intermissions became like gold dust! I had to spend every second doing something worthwhile. And that's actually how this book came to be written. This book is comprised of about 562 fifteen-minute intermissions in which I'd drive my room-mates crazy with the sound of my fingers tap-tap-tapping away at my keyboard.

When I look backwards and into my vault, the time I've wasted is just one of the many things I worry about. The stupid mistakes I made are another. No matter how well I've learned from those mistakes, they still created rifts between my friends and me and made my loved ones think less of me. It's like those "permanent records" you hear about on high school TV shows. You make a big mistake in school and it goes on your permanent record—except when you make a mistake in real life, it goes on the permanent record of your *life*, which is far harder to forget. You get to escape school after a certain amount of time but there's no escaping life, really. So, how do you make peace with that? Apologize, I've found. Doing all that you possibly can to rectify your mistake and putting the ball entirely in the court of whoever you've done wrong. I write letters. That's my way of doing it at least.

People who I've not spoken to in years suddenly receive a lengthy handwritten letter from me, explaining that I've realized I was a bit of an arse at one point or another in our friendship/relationship, and that I apologize from the bottom of my heart. Often I see if they want to meet for coffee, my treat, to end the letter, and if they get in touch it's usually a sign that the friendship can be renewed from that point onward, leaving the past where it is. If they don't accept, I still know I did all I could to explain and apologize, hoping that's enough to put their minds at rest, even if the friendship went through too many trials and tribulations in the past for them to want to put things back together again. I do realize I've made it sound like I'm a disaster area when it comes to friendships and that I've done awful things that need a lot of rectifying, which isn't the case at all—and I hope my friends agree! I think it's just that, when you realize the mistakes you've made and how you've made people feel, even if it was just for a split second and even if they can't remember it all these years later, it still makes you feel awful and it spurs you on to go to great lengths to apologize for things that maybe no one, actually, really cares about any more. Sort of like Ebenezer Scrooge in *A Christmas Carol* when he wakes up on Christmas morning and buys out the entire toystore and a mahoosive Christmas turkey and doles out gifts and favors to all those he's been miserly to! I don't have the funds to give gifts to everyone, but hopefully a heartfelt letter holds enough sentimental and emotional value that I'm forgiven the absence of pressies.

We all deal with things differently, and it's hard not to dwell on what has been but, all in all, the show must go on!

We have to find a way to put things in the past or our futures start to suffer and that's not cool, bro! So, my own personal rules for putting the past behind me are:

- Procrastinate less so that everything looks shinier in your vault.
- Do all you can to right the wrongs and accept the results, whether they're desired or not!

51

#AskCarrie

MY SOCIAL MEDIA FEEDS AND INBOXES are often filled with questions. Not just about my favorite Disney movies and how I take my tea, but also about the *real* stuff. Friends, bullying, stress, peer pressure, family, love, fitting in, and much, much more! I try to answer as best I can but, hey, I don't know it all! But I can offer the same kind of help and advice that any big sister, who's a few steps ahead in life, can offer. Seeing as you've all been on this journey with me up until now, why shouldn't you also be a part of this book? So, for a week I held a competition, of sorts, where you could submit your questions to be answered by me in this very book you're holding now! And guess what? Over four thousand of you submitted questions! I then went through each and every one of those questions with the help of a team at Little, Brown (my publisher in the UK), and narrowed it down to the twelve questions in this chapter. I tried to make sure I picked questions that would hopefully help a lot of people should they read them, and that there was a variety of topics covered. So, without further ado, here are my answers to your questions!

What helps you when you feel like everything is becoming too overwhelming? I imagine you've probably had a few overwhelming moments, with Les Mis *and YouTube and a BOOK (congratulations btw), so I'd love to know how you cope with it all. I'm currently about a month away from finishing high school so I'll have already graduated by the time your book is published (more time to read it, yay), but maybe it would help someone feeling a bit like I am now!*

You are totally right! Every now and then I do get a little overwhelmed by the amount of things I have to do at once. I'm awful for taking on too much work at the same time and getting myself in a muddle! I've found that taking things day by day is the key. If I'm always thinking about what I've got to do tomorrow and in a week's time and in a month's time, I start to get myself all worried about things that aren't going to be here for ages and then I'm less focused on the task at hand. So, I write out exactly what I need to do on a given day, in the order they need to be done, and just get through them one by one, trying to focus on one at a time and not worry about the next thing on the list! It takes willpower to force yourself to focus on just one thing in the moment and, for me, the urge to start multitasking and try to mix and match things on the list is sometimes overwhelming in itself. It takes a while to fight that instinct, but once you get used to just doing things in bite-sized chunks, it becomes easier to digest.

When most people think of the term "friend-zoned," it is normally assumed that it's worse for the person who is being rejected as more than a friend, which may be true. However on the other side I think it's quite bad as well. Speaking from experience, I feel very guilty and sad for not wanting to be more than friends with a good guy. My question is, do you have any advice on how to make both sides of the friend-zone feel better about the decision that was made?

I have a lot of thoughts on the idea of the "friend zone" and, looking at the comments on the video I made on the subject, so does everyone else! The term "friend zone," for those that don't know, is used to describe the situation in which two people are friends, but one person has developed romantic feelings for the other person and wants the friendship to develop into something more. Lots of people often say that this is just "unrequited love" but I disagree—I think they are two very different things. Unrequited love is exactly that. *Unrequited.* Meaning that you've already expressed your feelings to said person and you *know* that they don't feel the same way. The term "friend zone" is reserved for the people who have started to develop feelings for someone who is already an established friend of theirs and have yet to express those feelings because they just don't know how to approach the subject. Whenever I've been in that situation (which has been a few times), I've become the best friend in the world. I'll do things for that friend in the hope that they'll magically develop feelings for me on their own and realize I'm perfect for them! I do nice things for them—give them Jelly Tots for no reason! Leave Post-It notes on their desk with happy things written on them. They're always on my radar should they ever need me. And because I don't know how they feel because I haven't had the lady-balls to approach it, I have no idea whether they've guessed it, whether they know, whether they feel the same way . . . and it all gets a bit . . . much. It consumes everything I do and it's ridiculous! I could just walk up to them and say, "Hey. I have feelings for you. More than friendship feelings. And I don't want to ruin our friend-ship, but it was going to eat me alive like an alien if I didn't tell you and find out if you felt the same way. If you don't, that's totally cool, but in that case, I need some time alone to get over those feelings before we start hanging out again. And if you do, wanna go for coffee?"

So, now that you know my feelings on the "friend zone," to answer your question, you have *nothing* to feel bad about. You can't help how you feel as much as he can't help how he feels! I think the best thing to do would be to talk about it with him. If he's a friend, tell him that you feel bad you don't feel the same way, and ask him if there's anything you can do that can make it easier. He may feel like he needs some time away from you to try to get over his feelings before he can return to the friendship and start hanging out normally again. But you must make it very clear that you don't feel the same way. There's nothing worse than keeping someone on your hook/being kept on the hook. If he has feelings for you, any kind of uncertainty you give him is hope that he'll cling to, and it won't allow him to get over his feelings properly. For instance, "I don't have feelings for you right now." That "right now"? That's hope. He may think, *Right now? That means she may have feelings for me one day. I'll hold out hope until then!* It's only two words for *you*, but for *him* it could mean another few months of secretly harboring feelings for you. Just make it very clear, but gently, that you just don't feel the same way and, because he's your friend, you want to try to make things as easy for him as possible so that you can both return to being friends ASAP. But remember, you have *nothing* to feel bad about. That is just how you feel and that's totally A-OK!

I was just wondering, how do I deal with feeling like people always stay for a moment, and then leave me behind? It seems like whenever someone needs help with problems in their life, such as relationship trouble, they come to me for help. However, after their life takes a turn for the better, they tend to gradually disappear out of my life.

I'd suggest not giving out *all* your help, effort, and advice to those you don't trust to value the friendship enough to return it. They're the sorts of people that the word "acquaintance" is reserved for. Of course, if someone's asking for help it's so hard not to run to their aid and, by all means, do help them if you want to, but don't let their problems consume your life until they're solved, especially if you don't think they're the sort of person who will stick around long enough to help you out when you need them! But you really need to know that when they don't stick around, it's not because of you. It's their problem that they're flaky and they obviously don't know a good friend if one bit them on the bum. (But please don't do that— that won't make you any friends. Trust me . . . I've tried!)

If you could "bake" your ideal best friend, what ingredients would you use?

One cup of loyalty
One cup of reliability
A tablespoon of consideration
A teaspoon of creativity
A splash of affection
A dash of punctuality
A pinch of humor

Cook in the oven at 180 degrees of heart-warming until golden brown and kiss them on the cheek to wake them up! *Voilà!*

All I Know Now

My friend has been going out with her boyfriend for over a year, but still speaks and flirts with other guys as "it's only a bit of fun." This annoys me greatly, especially as one of the guys she speaks to I used to like. Her boyfriend doesn't know, and it is in no way my place to tell him, but I just feel so bad for him. I don't understand why she continues to seek this attention when she already has someone in her life, someone that a lot of us are looking for. I just wondered what your thoughts were on this.

I understand your frustration. It's hard to see someone act so casually with something special, and I get that sometimes it feels like they may take what they have for granted when other people crave it. But the thing is, it's totally OK that she speaks to other guys! I'd even go as far to say it's OK if she appears to flirt with them, because the thing about flirting is that a lot of the time you don't really realize you're doing it. You may think she's flirting, but to her it may just be witty, fun banter between two people who seem to connect well and which doesn't mean a thing. Flirting can mean more to the people doing it if they suddenly start meaning what they say, although that's hard to tell when you're looking in from the outside. If it makes you feel *really* uncomfortable, it may be worth talking to your friend. Let her know you've noticed her flirting and you're just a little worried that maybe her boyfriend might not appreciate it if he knew. But the fact she speaks to boys other than the one she calls her boyfriend shouldn't automatically be cause for alarm. If there are issues in her relationship that are causing her to look elsewhere, be there for her, but remember that, at the end of the day, it's really between her and her fella.

How do you get over someone who really hurt you? Last year I was in an emotionally manipulative (because abusive still sounds too real and makes me feel guilty) relationship that really shook my confidence, hurt me mentally, and continues to scare me. It wasn't the usual relationship or the typical break-up. This boy has really changed the way I think and am able to approach new people and, for want of a more eloquent term, he proper screwed me up. How do you move on from this? How do you teach yourself to accept the weight of the situation and then keep growing?

I was recently with a guy who "proper screwed me up" too and trust me when I say, boy do I know how that sucks! The main thing (and, in some cases, hardest thing) is to cut that person out of your life. Entirely. Delete numbers, social media profiles, and even pictures from your phone. It took me a long time to do it but when I did, suddenly . . . it felt like a weight had been lifted. I didn't have to worry about what they were doing or how they were making me feel because they didn't have the access to make me feel that way anymore. It's incredibly freeing, and I found the weight of the situation became less and less as the days moved further away from the point that he was in my life. There will be memories of course, but, if you're anything like me, it'll get to a point where it feels like it didn't happen to you. You'll get to a point where you are such a different person, a happier and more carefree person, that who you were in your relationship doesn't even feel like it *was* you anymore. Use what happened to make you stronger. Use those experiences with him to recognize the same situation if it ever arises again and stop it before it escalates to another manipulative relationship.

From the point that you cut him out onward, it's all about you for a while. Date yourself (there's a whole chapter on this earlier in the book!) and discover who you are, unattached to anyone else. Without anyone else's influence. See friends who you haven't seen in a long time. Go see movies you've not seen yet. Have dinner with just you and a notebook. Get to know who you are, unfiltered and undiluted.

You will be totally fine. Sometimes, when it's all happening, it feels like the Dementors have descended and there will never be happiness in your life again but, trust me, there will come a day when you are SO happy that you'll look back and it won't even feel like it ever happened to you, because you're so different and so much better off now. You've just gotta hold out through the crappy bits until that day comes.

Do you believe that a guy should always be the one to make the first move?

Ahh, that is the tradition, isn't it? I'd almost forgotten with the amount of guys I've asked out on dates! No, I don't think the guy should always be the one to make the first move. Personally, I feel it all depends on individuals and not genders. I'm a very forward person and I've dated guys who are quite shy, so in those cases I've made the first move because I know that even though they felt the same way I did, they were too shy and too embarrassed to ask me out. I also know a few guys who aren't shy but find it very attractive when a girl asks them out. It's all about reading the situation, reading the individual, and communicating with the other person. If you ask someone out, the worst-case scenario is that they say no and, guess what, the world keeps turning. But the best-case scenario is they say yes and you get to go on a date with someone you're obviously into because you asked them out, and someone who's obviously into you because they said yes! So the risk is definitely worth it. Male or female, it doesn't really matter! If you fancy someone and you want to ask them out, go for it!

I would never change who I am. I love when my friends come to me for help; but it seems like once their problems are fixed, they don't need me any more, and they leave. Please help; I'm not sure how to stop feeling like this.

It sucks when people do that! It always makes you feel like you're only good to rant at and solve your friends' problems but when it comes down to you and your own feelings and issues, suddenly everyone's sod off! I can completely relate to that. A while ago, a friend of mine didn't return my messages after I'd helped them out with a crisis. I was now asking them to go for coffee with me as I needed a shoulder to lean on, and when I talked to a theater colleague about this, she asked me, "Do you just . . . collect broken people, fix them, and then send them on their way?"

> Being uniquely imperfect is what makes us all interesting and what makes us all us.

I think it's a huge compliment that people trust you enough to come to you with their problems. They obviously see you as a very loyal, reliable, and trustworthy person, so definitely be flattered by that! But disappearing afterwards . . . that's not about you. That's about them. They've already established that they think you're a good, reliable friend by turning to you when things go wrong, but they haven't proven to be as reliable when it's time to return the favor. There will be people in your life who will have no issues in helping you when you need them, but it takes a while to find those people. They're rare—trust me! I'm twenty-two, and I've only got two friends from school who have stuck with me through everything, but everyone else up until now has left my life as quickly as they came into it. It's only really now that I'm understanding what it is I want from a friendship, and who in my life is offering that and asking the same thing from me in return. And it's also only now that I've started to find more of those people, now that I know exactly who I'm looking for.

So, trust me, you are not the reason they leave, and they probably don't even realize they've drifted away from you after you've helped them! It may be worth reminding those friends that you're there and that part of friendship is being there for *each other.*

Society in general and the local community surrounding me seem to crave perfection. To have perfect grades, be pretty, be fit, be thin, have a huge amount of friends, and have the most awesome social life in miles—and of course show that you are and have all these things by staying updated on all the social medias out there. And meanwhile staying on top of things and taking care of yourself. More importantly, so many of the people I surround myself with seem to have all these things and manage it all. I tried to manage it all, and for a good long while I did, got perfect grades, worked out five times a week. Until I just couldn't do it any more, was totally burned out. Managed to get myself half a cup of eating disorder and just a tablespoon of depression and anxiety too! I'm better now, but I've been out of school a lot, and starting the new semester is so scary—especially with "everyone" around me seemingly being able to balance it all: work, friends, school, exercise, family . . . All in all, in this world that seems to idolize perfection so much, do you have any tips on how to manage everyday life, balance things when you have a lot on your schedule, and being OK with not being perfect?

Personally, I don't believe perfection exists. People are far too complicated for everything to go right all the time, and I think that's worth remembering when you look at someone's *seemingly* perfect life. There will always be something you don't see that isn't perfect and isn't something you'd want to trade your own life for. People often think I live the perfect life based on what they see on social media, but they don't see the stressful nature of my job, how run down I get after months' worth of shows and concerts, the arguments I sometimes get into with family and friends, the way I look when I wake up in the morning, dealing with hate and negativity from people online . . . just because all that's not out there for everyone to see doesn't mean it doesn't exist! So, for every person you think is perfect, there are so many little imperfections behind closed doors that they don't want you to see. And rightly so! That's their private life that they don't have to share.

It's amazing that you've got such high standards for yourself and big ambitions, but perfection is an impossible standard that no one could ever reach no matter how hard they try! Balance is the key. Don't overwork yourself. Set small tasks for yourself to complete every day, but don't forget to give yourself time to relax, and don't give yourself such a hard time when something doesn't go quite according to plan. Most of all, stop comparing yourself to other people. Like I said, there will be hundreds of things about that person that you can't see that, if you *could* see, you'd probably never want to trade with them, because they're just as complicated and imperfect as you are!

Your idea of perfect could be very different from my idea of perfect so . . . what even is perfection anyway, really? Being uniquely imperfect is what makes us all interesting and what makes us all us. So, concentrate on you and what you want to achieve. Not on being somebody else and what everyone *expects* you to achieve!

My sister is so talented in so many ways—she's clever, she sings, she writes books and songs, she's amazing at art, and she has an amazing figure. I feel as if I'm under pressure to be like her, and to work out as much as she does. I know that she's going to do so well in life, and I feel as if I'm going to be a letdown if I don't do as well. How do I keep up to her standards and not feel as if I'm in her shadow the whole time?

Don't let your sister set your standards! You aren't her and that's wonderful. You are *you* and, sure, there may be things your sister has that you don't, but there are things that you have that your sister doesn't! You may be related but that doesn't mean you have to be identical to her and follow exactly in her footsteps. My brother is in a famous British band but . . . I've never had any desire to be in a band. Sure, we both perform for a living, but that's because I also love perform-ing. I didn't do it for him; I did it for me. But just because I perform in front of fewer people than he does every night, that doesn't mean that I'm a letdown! I found something I love doing, and I'm living my life how I want to live it, not how my brother lives his life and not how anybody else wants me to live my life. Find things that YOU enjoy doing and be who *you* want to be. That alone should make those around you happy but, more importantly, it needs to make *you* happy. Because what would be the point of living a life that you feel you *have* to live to make everyone else happy, when it makes you miserable, eh? Also, the more you feel like you're competing with your sister, the less healthy it gets for your sisterly relationship! Set your own standards, live your own life, and be proud of how well your sister is doing. And when you feel like you've found your feet and your passion in life, let her be proud of you too!

What is success? Is it defined by money, friends, intelligence? Is it something everyone must decide for themselves or is it something else?

Some people will define success by how much money they've earned in a year. Others will base it on how much they learned. Some will use their social media stats to show their success. Personally, my own success changes depending on what job I'm doing at the time. Currently, I'm playing Éponine in *Les Mis*, so I define my success based on how many shows I will have done by the end of my run (which should be around five to six hundred!) and the lovely feedback I get from the audience each night! I think it's something we all get to decide for ourselves. There are people whose definition of success in life is to have children and anything besides that is a bonus, yet there are those who never want children and find their own success in owning a business. Everyone wants to do something different with their lives, so having one blanket definition for success seems a little unfair and unforgiving. I believe you define your own success, and if someone tells you you haven't succeeded based on their own definitions and not yours then you need not listen!

Carrie, are you of the belief, with all the good and bad things that have happened to you in your life, that what doesn't kill you makes you stronger?

I am very much of that belief, yes! Everyone will go through trying times in their life. Rough patches. Bumps in the road. And I believe that if you don't let them defeat you, you can only learn from them, so when you're out the other side, you've grown as a person. You're wiser and better off for having been through those crappy times and, should the same situation arise again, you'll know how to deal with it. If it doesn't kill you, you can use it to grow and become better, wiser, and stronger.

Finale

SO HERE WE ARE. At the end of the book! Blimey. For a while there I didn't think we were gonna make it! It's been a pleasure to chat to you, and hopefully now that you've read about all my mistakes and the lessons I've learned, you feel a little better knowing that you're not alone? OR you think I'm the biggest moron to ever walk the earth and you're hoping to God you never have the misfortune to meet such a cretinous creature as me. But I dearly hope that's not the case!

Life is a strange thing. Sometimes we think we're heading one way and we're so sure of our future, and then quicker than you can say "I AM SO HAPPY RIGHT NOW" life decides to spin you round and round until you're so dizzy that you've fallen over and don't know which way is upside down. But you gotta keep going. You *have* to! The way I always think of it is: If I don't get up now, then I'm not giving the universe any reason to finally give me something good. If I don't get up and carry on going, I don't get to *make* anything good happen for myself. So, when I've been knocked over brutally, by George, I'm not just gonna sit here and dwell on the crappy stuff! I'm gonna stand on my two size-eight feet and, despite all the odds, I'm going to keep walking forward, even if it's in the wrong direction. It's better than not walking anywhere at all and I'll *make* something good happen. I'll sniff out that goodness somehow and then hold on to it with all my might!

We all go through crappy times when we think giving up is the only option. When we feel like the *Harry Potter* Dementors have sucked all the happiness out of our world and we'll never ever get it back again. Like a light switch has been flicked off and we have to guess our way around for a while. But what we all have to remember is that we're not the only person in all of space and time who has felt this way before, nor will we be the last. And that means there are happy people in this world who have been through what we're going through, and they've *survived*. They've come out the other side and they're smiling and living good lives, and that means we can do that too. It's not impossible. It's just hard. But still possible.

Being a teenager sometimes feels impossible. Some of the hardest things we face in our lives appear in our teen years, which hardly seems fair seeing as we're all so young to have to deal with it. But I suppose it's those crappy situations that make us learn exactly who we are and who we want to be, and the best time to learn is when you're still young and still developing yourself as a person. The best time to make mistakes is while you're still young enough to rectify them. When you're a puppy learning new tricks. Sure, you'll poop on the carpet, but your parents will shout at you and you'll learn not to do that again. (I'm running with the puppy analogy here . . . I hope none of you have *actually* pooped on your parents' carpet?)

I sincerely hope, having gotten this far in the book, you guys feel a little less alone and a little more prepared to face not only the big world out there (containing a few nasty people who want to squash our hopes and dreams) but also those voices in our own heads that tell us we aren't good enough.

Those voices are sometimes the toughest to ignore because they come from within and creep up on us when we least expect it, and because they're our *own* voices it's so hard to make them shush. But I'm hoping that when those voices start to natter away quietly in the back of our minds, there are a few chapters in this book that you can turn back to, to reassure yourself that you're not alone and you *can* pull through it and come out the other side far stronger than you ever could have imagined yourself to be.

Good luck!

Carrie
xxx

Props

If you are struggling with any of the issues I've talked about in this book, or with anything else that feels overwhelming, or you just want to talk to someone, please make use of the resources below. I hope they help.

First off, don't forget about your family doctor! Your doctor can be a really good place to start if you're trying to deal with a problem (physical or psychological) and are feeling a bit overwhelmed. If you don't feel comfortable talking to the same doctor who treats your parents, or if your doctor's a man and you'd rather speak to a woman, just ask the receptionist to make you an appointment with someone else. You can also ask your doctor to explain your right to confidentiality before you speak to them if that would make you feel more comfortable.

For further information about confidentiality and your rights, you can also call the General Helplines listed below for your area.

Below, I have included links to many helpful organizations in the USA and Canada, but unfortunately I can't list *all* the brilliant organizations out there or this book would be twice as long! If you need help or advice and can't find anything local listed below, then you can ask your doctor or school counselor to recommend a suitable organization—and a lot of the advice provided on these websites will be relevant and helpful no matter where you live. All of these links will be available on alliknownow.com, and if you would like to recommend any services that you've found useful, then please do so in the comments and perhaps you'll help out a fellow reader!

I've done my best to give correct information for all the resources listed here, but of course things like operating hours can change. Please check the websites of the listed organizations for the most up-to-date info. If you find that something in this section has gone out of date, please email info@theexperimentpublishing.com to let my publisher know. Thank you!

GENERAL HELPLINES

You can call these services (or text, or chat . . .) for help with any problem that has you overwhelmed. Family issues, relationships, LGBTQ topics, bullying, abuse, thoughts of self-harm, eating disorders, depression . . . you name it! There are also some topic-specific helplines in the sections that follow. I hope you find the perfect one for your needs!

United States

YOUR LIFE, YOUR VOICE   yourlifeyourvoice.org

Your Life, Your Voice is a free, 24-hour teen crisis hotline. If you need someone to talk to—about anything at all—please contact them to speak with an experienced counselor who can help. Spanish-speaking counselors and translation services representing more than 140 languages are available. Also, visit their website to read tips and posts from other users!

Call (800) 448-3000 (7 days a week, 24 hours a day).

To speak using a teletypewriter (TTY or TDD), call (800) 448-1833.

Text VOICE to 20121 (7 days a week, 6 pm to midnight CST).

Visit their website to speak by chat (Mon–Fri, 6 pm to midnight CST), or submit a question by email anytime.

TEEN LINE   teenlineonline.org

TEEN LINE is a confidential helpline for teenage callers. The TEEN LINE volunteers, who receive special training, are teenagers themselves. No problem is too small, too large, or too shocking—they are ready to listen to you and help sort through your options. At their website, you can connect with other users on the message boards and search the "Youth Yellow Pages" for additional resources near you!

Call (310) 855-4673 (7 days a week, 6 pm to 10 pm PST).

In California, call (800) 852-8336.

Text TEEN to 839863 (7 days a week, 5:30 pm to 9:30 pm PST).

Visit their website to submit a question by email anytime.

Canada

KIDS HELP PHONE   kidshelpphone.ca/teens

Don't be put off by "kids"! This is a free, 24/7 helpline with professional counseling for anyone up to 20 years old. Please contact them if you need to talk to someone, or if you need help finding other resources near you. You can also visit the "teens" part of their website to read other users' posts in the Express Yourself forums, and for information about a wealth of topics that might be worrying you!

Call (800) 668-6868 (7 days a week, 24 hours a day).

Visit their website to speak by chat (Wed–Sun, 6 pm to midnight EST), or submit a question to "Ask Us Online" anytime.

GENERAL ADVICE AND SUPPORT

REACH OUT   us.reachout.com

Check out all three parts of Reach Out's website: "The Facts" is full of helpful fact sheets on all the key topics of the Teen Age, written by teens and edited by a mental health professional. "Real Stories" are submitted by teens and young adults who have grappled with tough times and overcome! And the forums (for ages 13–24) are a great place to connect with others who are going through the same things you are. Also, don't miss the videos under "We Can Help Us"!

THE HOPEFULS FORUM   thehopefuls.freeforums.net

This is the official forum for my Hopefuls, which I started in 2014 so we all have a place to work through things together! The Hopefuls Forum might not be the right starting place for you if you need expert advice or urgent help—but if you are looking for a caring community of fellow Hopefuls who are eager to swap stories and offer support, you'll have come to the right place! Be sure to register and log in so you can see the full content of the forums.

HEALTH INFORMATION

CENTER FOR YOUNG WOMEN'S HEALTH
youngwomenshealth.org

The Center for Young Women's Health works to help teen girls and young women understand normal health and development, as well as specific conditions, so they can take an active role in their own care. Visit their website to search their helpful Health Guides on every topic imaginable, including sexual and emotional health. You can also submit a question to their weekly "Ask Us" feature, or visit them at the Boston Children's Hospital.

YOUNG MEN'S HEALTH   youngmenshealthsite.org

If you thought that last site sounded good, but you're a young man, you're in luck! Young Men's Health is a sibling site to the Center for Young Women's Health. Check it out for information you can trust on any health topic, including sexual or emotional health, or submit a question to their weekly "Ask Us" feature.

TEENS HEALTH   kidshealth.org/teen

This is another helpful website (including a Spanish-language section) about a wealth of health topics for teens, plus subjects like sports safety, test preparation, and even recipes for different health needs. All the articles are reviewed by a panel of physicians! Check out the Q&A section in particular for thoughtful answers about sex and relationships, depression and self-injury, body image, and more.

GIRLS HEALTH   girlshealth.gov

This website offers girls reliable, useful information on health and well-being. It covers a wide range of topics, from fitness to relationships, periods, drugs, bullies, careers, disability, self-esteem, and more.

Canada

Most Canadian provinces offer a free and confidential number you can call with non-emergency health questions—which includes health questions teens may feel a bit timid about asking someone in person. A registered nurse is available to take your call, provide advice and information, and direct you to the appropriate type of care. Services are provided in English, French, and more than 120 other languages. Remember that this service does not replace 911, which is always the first number to call in an emergency.

Alberta, British Columbia, New Brunswick, Newfoundland and Labrador, Nova Scotia, Prince Edward Island, Québec, Saskatchewan, or the Yukon

Call 811 (7 days a week, 24 hours a day).

To speak using a teletypewriter (TTY or TDD), call 711.

Manitoba

Call (888) 315-9257 (7 days a week, 24 hours a day).

Northwest Territories*

Call (800) 661-0844 (7 days a week, 24 hours a day).

Nanavut*

Call (800) 265-3333 (7 days a week, 24 hours a day).

Ontario

Call (866) 797-0000 (7 days a week, 24 hours a day).

To speak using a teletypewriter (TTY or TDD), call (866) 797-0007.

*The numbers listed here for the Northwest Territories and Nanavut are general helplines. Though your call may not be answered by a registered nurse, it will be answered by an informed and caring individual who is ready to listen and support you through any problem, and to help you find resources in your comujnity. Between 7 pm and midnight, the Nanavut number will be answered by someone with additional training and knowledge about sexual health, HIV/AIDS and other STDs, and contraception.

SEX, RELATIONSHIPS, AND SEXUAL ASSAULT: Helplines

If you have been a victim of unwanted sexual contact—regardless of whether the perpetrator was a stranger, friend, relative, or someone you're dating—you can call 911 and report it to the police. Your body is yours, and no one can touch it without your permission. If they do, that's a crime.

United States

RAPE, ABUSE, AND INCEST NATIONAL NETWORK (RAINN)
rainn.org

RAINN's mission is to help victims of sexual assault or abuse. Their trained staff members are available to listen, counsel, and provide information and referrals, via the National Sexual Assault Hotline (phone) or the National Sexual Assault *Online* Hotline (secure chat). You can contact them for yourself or if you are concerned about how to help a friend! You can also search their website for local support centers near you.

Call (800) 656-4673 (7 days a week, 24 hours a day).

Visit online.rainn.org to speak by chat (7 days a week, 24 hours a day).

LOVE IS RESPECT **loveisrespect.org**

Love Is Respect offers free and confidential peer counseling to young people who have questions or concerns about their dating relationships. The peer advocates who answer calls, texts, and live chats want to empower youth to prevent and end dating abuse. All of their services are available 7 days a week, 24 hours a day.

Call (866) 331-9474.

Text LOVEIS to 22522.

Visit their website to speak by chat.

NATIONAL DOMESTIC VIOLENCE HOTLINE   thehotline.org

Abuse in relationships can take more than one form, including physical or sexual violence, threats and intimidation, or emotional abuse. This is a free and confidential hotline that victims or those concerned about them can call for crisis intervention, safety planning, information, and referrals to local support agencies. Services are available in English and Spanish.

Call (800) 799-7233 (7 days a week, 24 hours a day).

To speak using a teletypewriter (TTY or TDD), call (800) 787-3224.

Visit their website to speak by chat (7 days a week, 7 am to 2 am CST).

Canada

For answers to sexual health-related questions, call the phone number listed for your province on page 321 under Health Information. Don't be shy! The nurse who takes your call will be happy to help you and won't think any question is too weird or embarrassing.

SEX, RELATIONSHIPS, AND SEXUAL ASSAULT: General Support

I WANNA KNOW!   iwannaknow.org

This is a website of the American Sexual Health Association (ashasexualhealth.org) that's especially for teens and young adults. Learn about relationships and sexual orientation, pregnancy and contraception, and STDs/STIs and how to prevent them. See the "Ask the Experts" section for Q&As or to submit your own question to their doctors and nurses.

IT'S YOUR (SEX) LIFE   itsyoursexlife.com

This site (a project of MTV) has answers to your questions about all things sex. And if it doesn't, it links to somewhere that does. Check out the "hotlines and resources" page if you find yourself in a pregnancy scare or any kind of sexual crisis—it's really thorough!

SCARLETEEN: SEX ED FOR THE REAL WORLD   scarleteen.com

Here you'll find straight-up, inclusive, and diverse sexuality information. This site is specifically geared toward teens and 20s. In addition to informative articles, it includes user-to-user and user-to-staff message boards, and advice columns.

In the United States, text questions to (206) 866-2279 for an answer within 24 hours.

Visit their website to speak with a member of the Scarleteam by chat (time windows vary by month).

TEEN TALK   teentalk.ca

This Canadian website *thoroughly* covers all topics sex-related (sexuality, sexual health, sexual assault, and more) and also touches on issues like mental health, body image, and substance use. Wherever you live, you can learn a ton from this site!

GO ASK ALICE!   goaskalice.columbia.edu

Go Ask Alice! is a public forum for health questions that has been run by Columbia University Health since 1993. It has an incredible archive of user-submitted Q&As. The sections on relationships and sexual health really stand out, and it also covers alcohol and other drugs, emotional health, and general health, fitness, and nutrition. (This one is *not* written just for teens, so please use your own judgment, as some of the content may push your comfort limits!)

LGBTQ

IT GETS BETTER PROJECT   itgetsbetter.org

The It Gets Better Project charts social change, communicates to lesbian, gay, bisexual and transgender youth around the world that it gets better, and inspires them to be loud and vocal in advocating for the changes that still need to be made. It's a place where people can share their stories and watch videos of love and support.

JUST LEFT THE CLOSET justleftthecloset.com

This is an anonymous social network (with made-up usernames) for LGBTQ youth and their friends. Whether you're still in, shyly emerging, proudly out, or just curious, you might enjoy reading others' stories and thoughts and posting your own!

TRANS LIFELINE translifeline.org

Trans Lifeline is a nonprofit hotline run by transgender people, for transgender people. (This includes people who may be struggling with their gender identity or who are not sure that they are transgender!) The volunteers are ready to help anyone in crisis or at risk of self-harm, or to respond to whatever support needs that members of the trans community might have.

In the United States, call (877) 565-8860 (7 days a week, 24 hours a day).

In Canada, call (877) 330-6366 (7 days a week, 24 hours a day).

United States

THE TREVOR PROJECT thetrevorproject.org

The Trevor Project is a support system and community for LGBTQ youth and allies. It includes a crisis-intervention phone service, non-emergency support via instant messaging and text, and Trevor-Space, a worldwide social network for LGBTQ youth and their friends (ages 13 to 24). Visit their website to join!

If you are experiencing thoughts of self-harm, call (866) 488-7386 (7 days a week, 24 hours a day).

For non-emergency support, text (202) 304-1200 (Fridays, 4 pm to 8 pm EST).

Visit their website to speak by chat (7 days a week, 3 pm to 9 pm EST).

Canada

For immediate help, call Kids Help Phone: (800) 668-6868. This free 24/7 helpline is for young people up to 20 years old (despite the name). Their professional counselors are trained to address concerns

that many LGBTQ youth may have. Read more on page 319 under
General Helplines.

ABUSE, BULLYING, AND ONLINE SAFETY
THE CHILDHELP NATIONAL CHILD ABUSE HOTLINE
childhelp.org/hotline
If you or someone you know is being abused or at risk of abuse, this confidential helpline will offer support and steer you toward additional help. You can call from the US, US territories, and Canada! All calls are answered by professional crisis counselors.

Call (800) 422-4453 (7 days a week, 24 hours a day).

Cyberbullying fact sheet:
nobullying.com/facts-about-cyber-bullying

REACH OUT **us.reachout.com/bullying**
This section of the Reach Out site offers advice on what to do if you are being bullied or you know someone who is. It also features fact sheets on different kinds of bullying (online, girl versus girl, and more), inspirational and informative videos, and personal stories from real teens who endured and overcame bullying. See more about Reach Out on page 319 under General Help and Support.

PREVNET **prevnet.ca/bullying/teens**
This site offers facts, solutions, and advice for people who are victims and witnesses of bullying, as well as for those who think they may have caused others harm. There are also sections dedicated to cyberbullying and issues that LGBTQ teens face.

To speak to a counselor about bullying, please consult the General
Helplines starting on page 318.

MENTAL HEALTH, SELF-HARM, AND SUICIDE

911 is the number you should call for immediate help in a crisis (in both the US and Canada).

IM ALIVE   imalive.org

If you, or someone you know, are having thoughts of self-harm, visit this site to chat online—anytime from anywhere in the US or Canada—with volunteers trained in crisis intervention.

United States

NATIONAL SUICIDE PREVENTION LIFELINE

suicidepreventionlifeline.org

This free and confidential suicide-prevention hotline provides crisis counseling and mental health referrals to anyone in emotional distress—day or night. You can also visit their website to chat with a counselor online, anytime.

Call (800) 273-8255 (7 days a week, 24 hours a day).

THE TREVOR LIFELINE

thetrevorproject.org/pages/get-help-now

This 24/7 lifeline is part of the Trevor Project, a support system for LGBTQ youth and allies. Please call them if you, or a friend, are having thoughts of self-harm. Read more about the Trevor Project on page 325 under LGBTQ.

Call (866) 488-7386 (7 days a week, 24 hours a day).

Canada

For immediate help, call Kids Help Phone: (800) 668-6868. This free 24/7 helpline is for young people up to 20 years old (despite the name) and will put you in touch with a professional counselor. Read more on page 319 under General Helplines.

CANADIAN ASSOCIATION FOR SUICIDE PREVENTION
suicideprevention.ca/thinking-about-suicide/
This website has a very complete listing of local crisis centers in Canada. Use it to search for the one nearest you, including 24-hour phone numbers you can call. (Please bear with the site even though it loads a bit slowly!)

YOUTH SPACE   youthspace.ca
At Youth Space, anyone under 30 who's going through a tough time can connect via chat or text with a volunteer counselor who is trained in emotional support and crisis response.

Text (778) 783-0177 (7 days a week, 6 pm to midnight PST).

Visit their website to speak by chat.

THE LIFELINE APP   thelifelinecanada.ca
This app puts Kids Help Phone (24/7 phone support) and YouthSpace .ca (text support) at your fingertips, plus a helpful map of local crisis centers all across Canada so you can find the one nearest you. You can download it for free from iTunes or the Android app store (visit the website for links).

Also see the below resources for specific provinces!

British Columbia
Mind Check (**mindcheck.ca**) is designed to help youth in British Columbia with anxiety, stress, alcohol and drugs, body image, and more. Visit their website to assess how you're feeling and quickly connect to mental-health resources and support.

British Columbia and Yukon
The volunteers at Youth in BC (**youthinbc.com**) are all in their twenties, and are ready to help you talk through anything—including bullying, disordered eating, drugs, alcohol, LGBTQ issues, mental health, sexual health, sexual assault, and thoughts of self-harm.

Call the YouthinBC crisis line at (866) 661-3311 (7 days a week, 24 hours a day).

Visit their website to speak by chat (7 days a week, noon to 1 am PST).

Ontario

If you are a post-secondary student in Ontario (age 17–25), visit Good2Talk (**good2talk.ca**) for free and confidential counseling, information, and referrals about mental health, addiction, or any issue that's affecting your well-being. Professional counselors are always ready to talk, in English or French.

Call (866) 925-5454 (7 days a week, 24 hours a day).

EATING DISORDERS

United States

THE NATIONAL EATING DISORDERS ASSOCIATION (NEDA)

nationaleatingdisorders.org

NEDA works to raise awareness of eating disorders (such as anorexia, bulimia, and binge eating disorder) and to provide families with programs and support. Visit their website to learn more and to find help. If you are struggling with an eating disorder or know someone who is, please call their free, confidential helpline.

Call (800) 931-2237 (Mon–Thu, 9 am to 9 pm EST;
and Fri, 9 am to 5 pm).

Visit their website to speak by chat (during the same times).

Canada

THE NATIONAL EATING DISORDER INFORMATION CENTRE (NEDIC)

nedic.ca

At the NEDIC website, you can learn more about eating disorders and treatment options, and search for local support centers near you. They also have a free, confidential helpline to call for information and support if you are struggling with an eating disorder or know someone else who is.

Call (866) 633-4220 (Mon–Fri 9 am to 9 pm EST).

In Toronto, call (416) 340-4156.

DRUGS AND ALCOHOL

ABOVE THE INFLUENCE   abovetheinfluence.com

The goal of Above the Influence is to encourage teens to stay true to themselves—instead of just going along with the crowd. See their website for the latest facts about drugs and alcohol (and depression), as well as pointers on coping with peer pressure in general. Experts answer FAQ, and teens contribute inspiring wall posts under "Speak Up!" The site also links to tons of resources where you can get help for yourself or for others.

United States

NIDA FOR TEENS   teens.drugabuse.gov

The National Institute on Drug Abuse (NIDA) created this fact-based website just for teens. Visit to learn more about the effects of different drugs on health and well-being, and to find advice if you think that you or someone you know might have a substance-abuse problem. Call their helpline to speak with a specialist who can answer your questions and connect you with local treatment facilities, support groups, and community organizations.

Call (800) 622-4357 (7 days a week, 24 hours a day).

Canada

All of the following websites and helplines are free and confidential. Their purpose is to provide basic education about drug and alcohol problems. Call the number listed for your province to reach someone who will listen, offer support, and provide strategies to help you or your loved one meet your goals. They can also refer you to treatment centers and support programs in your area.

Alberta

Call (866) 332-2322 (7 days a week, 24 hours a day).

Visit albertahealthservices.ca/amh.asp

British Columbia

Call (800) 663-1441 (7 days a week, 24 hours a day).

From the Lower Mainland, call (604) 660-9382.

Visit heretohelp.bc.ca

Manitoba

Call (877) 710-3999 (Mon–Fri, 7:30 am to 4:30 pm CST).

To speak using a teletypewriter (TTY or TDD), call (204) 958-9685.

After hours, call the Youth Mobile Crisis Team at (204) 949-4777 (7 days a week, 24 hours a day).

Visit gov.mb.ca/healthyliving/addictions/youth.html

Nanavut

Call (800) 265-3333 (7 days a week, 24 hours a day).

Visit gov.nu.ca/health/information/substance-abuse

New Brunswick

Call (866) 524-6199 (7 days a week, 24 hours a day).

Visit gnb.ca/0378/addiction-e.asp

Newfoundland and Labrador

Call 811 for information and medical advice (7 days a week, 24 hours a day).

If you are in crisis, call (888) 737-4668 (7 days a week, 24 hours a day).

To find a treatment facility, visit health.gov.nl.ca/health/mentalhealth

Nova Scotia

Call (866) 340-6700 (Mon–Fri, 8:30 am to 4:30 pm AST).

After hours, call (866) 524-6199 (7 days a week, 24 hours a day).

Visit novascotia.ca/dhw/addictions/addiction-services-offices.asp, or visit gethelpstopping.ca

Northwest Territories

Call (800) 661-0844 (7 days a week, 24 hours a day).

Visit hss.gov.nt.ca/social-services/mental-health-and-addictions/addictions-where-get-help

Ontario

Call (800) 565-8603 (7 days a week, 24 hours a day).

Visit drugandalcoholhelpline.ca

Prince Edward Island

Call (888) 299-8399 (7 days a week, 24 hours a day).

Visit healthpei.ca/addictions

Québec

Call (800) 265-2626 (7 days a week, 24 hours a day).

Visit drogue-aidereference.qc.ca

Saskatchewan

Call (866) 524-6199 (7 days a week, 24 hours a day).

Visit canadadrugrehab.ca/Saskatchewan-Alcohol-Drug-Rehab-Programs.html

Yukon

Call (855) 667-5777 (7 days a week, 24 hours a day).

Visit hss.gov.yk.ca/ads.php

Curtain Call

IT'S TAKEN A LONG TIME TO WRITE THIS BOOK, and it couldn't have been completed without the help, love, and support of some very brilliant and important people, and this silly page in the back of a book that no one really reads will do no justice to how much gratitude they're owed!

Firstly, everyone at Little, Brown Book Group who had to put up with my daft requests and suggestions! Especially Hannah Boursnell, Sarah Shea, Rhiannon Smith, Stephanie Melrose, Hannah Wood, and Sara Talbot . . . thank you for always having cake and tea at the ready when I visited during the process of making this book and for all your love and enthusiasm. You're all utterly brilliant and it's been a pleasure! A massive thank you to my wonderful book agent Hannah Ferguson! Thank you for believing in my potential as a writer and just being an all round lovely person. I couldn't ask for anyone better at my side! Also, to everyone at Curtis Brown! You've been hugely supportive over the last couple years. I can't tell you how much I appreciate how much you've done for me. And of course, Marc Samuelson. Without you, the path to where I am now would never have been found and it was your pure faith in me that lead me there.

Secondly, my mum and dad, Bob and Debbie Fletcher. Without them I wouldn't have made it through the Teen Age, let alone been able to write a book about it. You're both mad and I Love You. Tom, my big brother. Thanks for helping me through my teenage years with such unconditional support and love, and for always laughing at my stupid jokes. Hope there's enough in this book to keep you going! My sister-in-law, Gi, a fellow author! Thank you for all your advice in the book world . . . and in the real world! You sisterly love for me is always overwhelmingly wonderful. Little Buzz Head! I hope there comes a time when Auntie Carrie's book comes in handy! But if you ever have any questions, I'll always be just around the corner! Thank you to my nan and granddad, Joan and Ken Richardson, for all the times you drove me to school and to various train stations. You've always helped me to get where I'm going, geographically and in life. And my cousin, Jojo, with whom I spent so much of my childhood and who I talk about in this book. We must be ***** twins! All my family have influenced this book in some way and I wish I had the space to name you all, but whether you're a Fletcher, Lamb, Shears, Carr, Reeder, Richardson, Boyce, or Ramsden, know that you're all loved! Thank you!

Thirdly, I'd like to thank Ray Lamb, my first singing teacher. You helped me, my voice, and my confidence in ways I doubt I can ever repay. Next time I see you, the Rolos are on me!

Thank you to everyone at "Hogwarts." My time with you was magical and I owe a lot to you. Namely, I'd like to thank Dr. Roche, not just for all your knowledge of music but for your friendship (not to mention all those lunchtimes you spent playing piano for me while I belted out songs from every musical the world has ever seen) and Mr. Brown, my

English teacher, for putting up with my enthusiasm which was hugely disproportionate to my intelligence. Look! I wrote a book! A WHOLE BOOK!

Fourthly, my friends, some of whom were written about in this book. Vicky Martinelli and Saffron Manning, you've put up with some serious silliness on my part. Thanks for sticking around! Lizzie Newbury, thanks for all the banana bread in school! Alan Cole, thanks for inspiring a chapter in this book! (But I'm not ever saying thank you for making me throw up!) Dayle Hodge, you're an idiot, but you're an idiot with a special place in my heart. Jack Howard, even though you're either late or you don't show up, thanks for occasionally having dinner with me and reminding me just how unstoppable us individuals can be. Rock 'n' Roll! Gary Caplehorne, thanks for *always* having my back and for being the sassiest person I know. Thank you to all the friends I made at Harrow School for all the times you sneaked me into your boarding houses and let me eat your takeaway food. You guys showed me what friendship really is. Thank you to all the inhabitants of The Queen's Theatre! You're like family! Namely Wendy Ferguson, Emilie Fleming, and Celinde Schoenmaker. Thank you for putting up with the clickety-clack of my keyboard in our tiny dressing room! *Ik hou van jou!* Anton Zetterholm, thank you for always looking so proud of me when I tell you what I've been up to. And Dougie Carter, you've been like my theater brother these last two years. Thank you for looking out for me!

And then there's Pete Bucknall. Oh, Pete. Thank you for being my Disney Prince. Now that we're technically adults you've taught me the important things in life like how to say

Prezzo, how to be "adorkable," and the best places in your car to hold on to for dear life when you're driving! But mainly, thank you for showing up when I needed you the most.

Last but certainly not least, The Hopefuls. You've all stuck by me through a lot, some of you for years now, and without you and everything you share with me, well, I wouldn't have written this book. Because you're who it's for. I hope you enjoyed it and I hope it has helped.

In case I've been unforgivably forgetful . . .

Thank you [insert name here]! You're brilliant and I couldn't have written this book without you!

Find Me Online!

YouTube	www.youtube.com/carrie
Twitter	@carriehfletcher
Facebook	www.facebook.com/itswaypastmybedtime
Instagram	@carriehopefletcher
Tumblr	www.carriehopefletcher.com
Blog	www.alliknownow.com

And let me know what you think about the book using #alliknownow

xxx

About the Author

CARRIE HOPE FLETCHER is an actress, singer, vlogger, and, thanks to her popular YouTube channel ItsWayPastMyBedtime, "honorary big sister" to hundreds of thousands of young people around the world. The videos she creates (on topics as diverse as exam stress, handling school bullies, and how to pee in a onesie) have been viewed more than fifty million times. She was one of seven finalists in the Actress category for the 2015 Shorty Awards.

Carrie is currently playing the role of Éponine in *Les Misérables* at the Queen's Theatre in London's West End, for which she received the 2014 WhatsOnStage Award for Best Takeover in a Role. She lives just outside London with numerous fictional friends that she keeps on the bookshelves, just in case.

All I Know Now is Carrie's first book. It has been a #1 bestseller in the *Sunday Times* (UK) and spent twelve weeks in the top ten. She is now writing her upcoming first novel, *On the Other Side*.